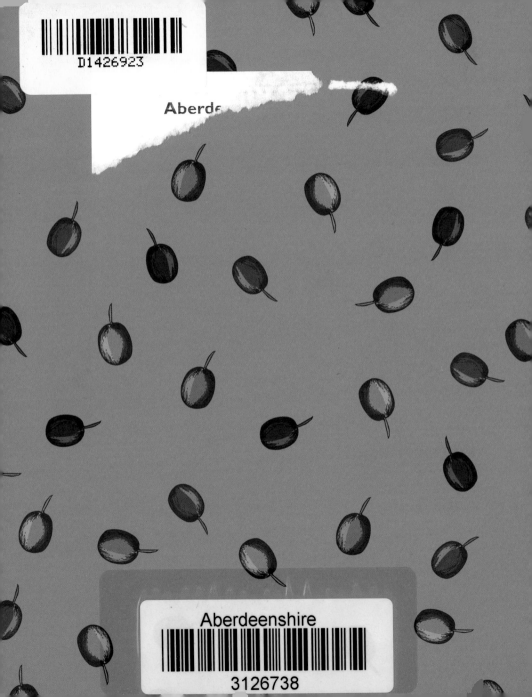

100 Plants
that almost changed the World

100 Plants
that almost changed the World

by **Chris Beardshaw**

design and illustration by Shirlynn Chui-Jacobs

First published in Great Britain in 2013 by Papadakis Publisher

An imprint of New Architecture Group Limited

Kimber Studio
Winterbourne
Berkshire, RG20 8AN, UK
info@papadakis.net
www.papadakis.net

   @papadakisbooks
   PapadakisPublisher
   PapadakisPublisher

Publishing Director: Alexandra Papadakis
Design and Illustration: Shirlynn Chui-Jacobs
Editor: Sheila de Vallée
Editorial Assistant: Juliana Kassianos

ISBN: 978 1 906506 19 3

Acknowledgement

My thanks must go to all those individuals
whose efforts and endeavours have helped
create these stories.

Their pioneering attitude, persistence and perseverance
in searching for knowledge and enlightenment
have overlapped with horticulture; at times the discoveries
have been unusual, perhaps unintentional
and in some cases completely inappropriate!

Their efforts result in an entirely personal,
arbitrary and slightly irreverent collection of tales
and facts that amuse and inspire me.

Dedication

To Florrie, Lily and Georgia –
long may you possess an endearing capacity
to remain unshackled by the mundane.

Contents

Commonly known as Salsify or Goatsbeard this plant of English wildflower meadows, hedgerows and ditches often grows uninvited in our gardens because of its regular inclusion in wild birdseed. Traditionally shunned on account of its strong salty flavour the plant is now undergoing something of a popularity boost thanks to adventurous chefs getting creative with the pungent root and putting it on their menus as a vegetarian alternative to oysters.

Agave is one of Mexico's favourite plants; the pulp of the foliage is the source of the nation's favourite drink, tequila. But now, fuelled by an extra incentive, the nation is rushing out to buy cheap bottles of it following scientists' claims that they have been producing synthetic diamonds from it.

To release the gems all that is necessary is to heat the liquid, collect the gas, break it into separate particles, increase the heat some more – to around 800°C – and collect the resulting carbon deposits.

Apparently the diamonds currently produced are perfect for abrasive and industrial cutting purposes. But if you are thinking of experimenting, be warned: the particles are only visible through an electron microscope. Still, it is, after all, the thought that counts!

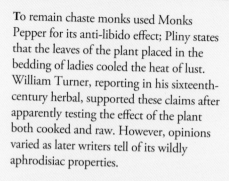

To remain chaste monks used Monks Pepper for its anti-libido effect; Pliny states that the leaves of the plant placed in the bedding of ladies cooled the heat of lust. William Turner, reporting in his sixteenth-century herbal, supported these claims after apparently testing the effect of the plant both cooked and raw. However, opinions varied as later writers tell of its wildly aphrodisiac properties.

The plant causing this controversy is *Vitex agnus-castus* a temperate relative of tropical and sub-tropical plants commonly referred to as the Chaste Tree. Research suggests both bickering parties are right, at least in part, although the effects are not clearly understood. The reaction seems to hinge on the precise amount of the herb consumed: high doses seem to reduce the levels of oestrogen in women and testosterone in men but take too little and the effects are dramatically reversed.

Contemporary medicine utilises the plant to stabilise hormones, and particularly for cyclical breast discomfort and premenstrual syndrome, for stabilising the menstrual cycle after withdrawal from progesterone birth control pills and for regulating ovulation. Thankfully it is no longer necessary to apply the herb in underwear.

As a modest symbol of the Alps, where it is now confined to limestone rock crevices, the Edelweiss is a high altitude specialist with an array of evolutionary tactics that enable it to thrive in extremes of temperature, savage winds and blistering ultraviolet light. Various nations have admired it: the Greeks observed that the composite flower bud resembled a lion's paw and gave us the name Leontopodium, while the Germans admired the plant's purity and audacity giving us the common name *'edel'* meaning noble and *'weiss'* meaning white.

During the Victorian era it was in such demand as a symbol of love, purity and devotion that the likelihood of seeing its woolly foliage, furry stems and creamy white, star-like flower today is remote as it is now confined to a few locations. It is officially both endangered and protected but still fails to excite outside its homeland. This is perhaps attributable to the unofficial adoption of the plant by the Third Reich, and the *Edelweisspiraten*, or Edelweiss Pirates, within its ranks.

Such setbacks are unfortunate as it has now been revealed that the inherent compounds in this diminutive specimen include chlorogenic acid, luteolin, apigenin, bisabolane and sitosterol, which combine to offer antioxidant, anti-inflammatory, antiseptic, antifungal and bactericidal properties. Such is the potency of the plant that many claim it is the ideal ingredient for the treatment of stressed and sensitive skin, particularly damage resulting from ageing.

For cleansing a magic circle, protecting the wearer against evil spells, assisting the passage of the dead into the after-life, repelling ants, fleas and flies, and generally assisting in the embalming of a body there are few better horticultural contenders than Tansy (*Tanacetum vulgare*). In addition to this sinister portfolio it is also highly toxic to all mammals and, in the universally adopted language of flowers, constitutes a declaration of war upon the recipient.

Today Tansy has been enlisted in the fight against pollutants as research suggests that in urban and industrial areas its unusually deep roots and unique structure cleanse the soil of heavy metals, especially lead and mercury, by locking them into inert compounds. Just remember not to compost the spent plant.

When western scientists tentatively examined an innocuous plant from Japan their interest was aroused when lab results indicated that a known active constituent, an amino acid called betaine was present in high quantities. In addition to betaine, it contained all ten amino acids considered essential to health. Subsequently, this previously ignored relative of the tomato, commonly called Goji Berry or Wolfberry has demonstrated an ability to protect the liver, reduce blood sugar levels and enhance the immune system via polysaccharides; the fruit is rich in linoleic acid needed for the construction of cell walls, also preventing fats from being deposited on blood vessel walls. Tannins present reduce inflammation while also containing vitamins A, B1, B2, and iron.

Science officially declared Goji (*Lycium chinense*) a 'Super Berry', only to find it occupied a prominent position in the oldest Chinese Herbal, *Sinnouhonzougyou* dating back over 1,800 years. According to this book, the fruits nourished the liver and kidney, and made an excellent tonic to combat fatigue, lumbago, dullness, vertigo, anaemia, and failing eyesight. The root bark was recommended to reduce fevers and it was said to enhance life forces and to rejuvenate. It also claimed that there was no finer gift presented at the Royal Courts.

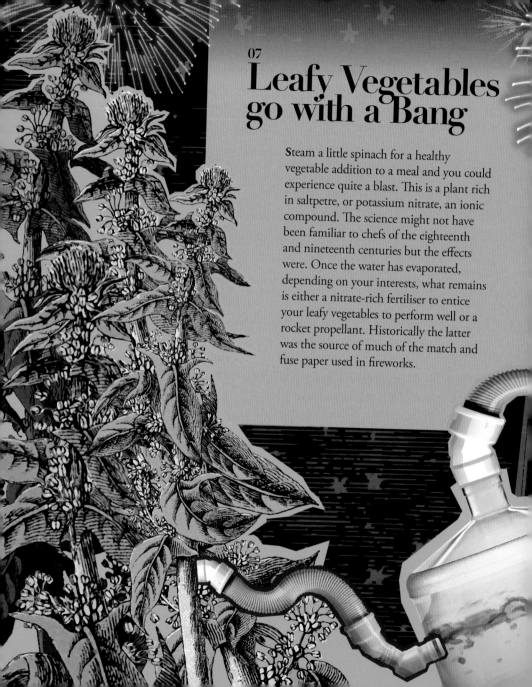

Leafy Vegetables go with a Bang

Steam a little spinach for a healthy vegetable addition to a meal and you could experience quite a blast. This is a plant rich in saltpetre, or potassium nitrate, an ionic compound. The science might not have been familiar to chefs of the eighteenth and nineteenth centuries but the effects were. Once the water has evaporated, depending on your interests, what remains is either a nitrate-rich fertiliser to entice your leafy vegetables to perform well or a rocket propellant. Historically the latter was the source of much of the match and fuse paper used in fireworks.

 08·Giving Geraniums a bad name

Cottage gardens filled with the sweet scent and heady fragrance of springtime blooms might portray a rural idyll but just imagine receiving an official Government leaflet informing you that 'if you smell Geraniums you're dead'.

This is exactly what happened to the residents of many cities in Britain during the Second World War. These were not comments on horticultural performance; there was, of course, no chance of Geraniums falling from the sky, but the fragrance is indicative of Blister Gas, suspected of being manufactured and used in bombing raids by the Luftwaffe. This organoarsenic compound is better known as mustard gas or lewisite and the fear of its use prompted 38 million gas masks to be issued to the British public. Ironically, many of the types of respirator issued would not have been effective against such a gas.

Ketchup was once sold as a medicine. In the 1830s general store owner Archibald Miles launched pills called 'Dr. Miles' Compound Extract of Tomato'. He sold them to more than 100,000 customers across the country before he was declared a fraud. What he was actually selling was based on an early recipe for ketchup, derived from Indonesian and Asian cuisine.

This spicy, pickled fish sauce made from anchovies, walnuts, mushrooms and beans was called ke-tsiap or kecap and was popular in seventeenth-century China.

British seamen are thought to have brought ke-tsiap home with them. The name was changed to catchup and then finally ketchup. It wasn't until the late 1700s that enterprising New Englanders thought to add tomatoes. The idea was picked up by one Henry J. Heinz in 1876 and he started to bottle the concoction for sale.

The modern interpretation is so removed from the original as to be unrecognisable, although the contemporary version out-performs the genuine article in stripping oxidised metal compounds from the outside of pots and pans.

In the mid-1700s, grapefruit was known as the Forbidden Fruit. It was so described by the Reverend Griffith Hughes, who was searching for the identity of the original tree in the Garden of Eden. In 1814, in his *Hortus Jamaicensis*, John Lunan described its taste as 'resembling the flavour of the grape'. Clearly he had never tasted one.

Quite why this succulent citrus fruit earned the name Grapefruit is debatable. It was first observed in Barbados where an Orange had been crossed with a larger relative called the Pummelo. The young fruits were borne in clusters along the branches and, when embryonic, resembled a bunch of grapes.

As the world's most popular fruit, apples are credited with an enviable lineage from the wild crab apples we see in our hedgerows to the wealth of delicious, succulent fruit in our fruit bowls. Until recently this seemed possible but new genetic findings from Italy have exploded the myth that all apples are derived from European wild forms. In fact, it is clear that a remote collection of trees found in the sparsely populated mountains of Kazakhstan and Uzbekistan are the real ancestor.

So genetically similar are these ancient trees that despite the passage of thousands of years they display all the varied characteristics of the modern forms and many are every bit as edible. It is not known quite how these apples travelled to the West but trade routes and animals are the main suspects for facilitating their journey. We know that the Greeks were cultivating several forms by 300 BC and that the crop spread throughout the Roman Empire. What complicates textual research is that, until recent history, almost any fruit carried by a tree was referred to as an Apple, including many that bear little or no resemblance to modern fruits. This begs the question as to whether the imposters were named after the Apple or was the term Apple simply used to describe any newly introduced fruit from the East.

The Watermelon has long been associated with ancient civilisations; it was a celebrated part of the Egyptian diet 5000 years ago and is depicted in the hieroglyphs that adorned the walls of their ancient monuments. Watermelons were even buried in the tombs of Egyptian kings in the belief that they would provide sustenance and nourishment in the afterlife.

A member of the Cucurbitaceae family, which includes the Cucumber and Pumpkin, the Watermelon is thought to have its origins in the Kalahari Desert of Africa. Richly fragranced and deliciously juicy it is easy to appreciate emerging civilisations being wowed by the fruits.

The seeds were traded along the Mediterranean coasts. The Chinese started cultivating it in the tenth century, and in the thirteenth century the Moors helped spread it throughout their empire. It was probably the African slave trade that resulted in the plant taking root in the New World.

At over 92% water the benefit of the fruit has conventionally been accepted as providing good hydration, but perhaps the Egyptians discovered an alternative interest.

Watermelon is now known to contain a wealth of beneficial compounds; these include lycopene, in higher quantities than in tomatoes, beta carotene, delivering vitamin A, and the stellar of phyto-nutrients, citrulline, whose beneficial functions are now becoming unlocked. When watermelon is consumed, citrulline is converted into arginine. Arginine is an amino acid that affects both heart and circulatory system. The arginine stimulates the release of nitric oxide, which in turn relaxes blood vessels; the net result is that watermelon could have much the same effect as Viagra.

Nutrients in the soils clearly affect the wellbeing of plants and when the function of these foods is understood a picture of some clarity emerges about the history of the soil. Of the three major nutrients for plant growth potassium is generally responsible for floral stimulation, nitrogen affects chlorophyll in the leaf, and phosphorous is critical as a stimulus for root growth and branching. When phosphorous is available to plant roots, early leaf growth and enhanced vigour ensue.

Combine this knowledge with an understanding of colonising plants such as the Nettle (*Urtica dioica*) and a remarkable tool presents itself in the investigation of genocide. The gruesome truth is that as the bodies of victims decompose phosphorous is slowly released; when this is taken up as a nutrient by plants such as the Nettle, significant anomalous growth is visible. When investigators and forensic archaeologists studied aerial photographs of suspected mass graves, the lush Nettle growth led them straight to the crime scene.

History demonstrates a more civilised understanding of a similar principle: the graves of monks and the upper classes were often located in orchards, thus ensuring giant trees and generous crops.

Thriving on the rocky lower slopes of the mountains in northwest China is a rarely reported tree, related to the Euphorbia that produces oil-rich seeds. It is known as the Tung Tree. Its seeds are heated, ground and pressed to release their precious oils, which are thin and transparent and penetrate deeply into the pores of wood on which it is painted, forming an almost permanent seal against moisture and never losing its elasticity. It was this property that was exploited by the Chinese as early as the fourteenth century to waterproof their ships.

It is used today as a quick-drying oil in the manufacture of the finest quality lacquers, varnishes and paints, and in linoleum, oilcloth, resins, artificial leather, floor coverings, greases, and cleaning and polishing compounds. It was also tried by the Chinese military as a diesel fuel alternative, until it was discovered that after repeated applications it caused engines to seize up.

¹⁵A Cry for Help

Watch a favoured plant being desecrated or devoured by marauding garden pests and it is easy to assume that it has few defence mechanisms. However, it is now known that when a plant is attacked it emits pheromones via its stomata, the tiny pores in the tissue through which gaseous exchange takes place. The pheromones drift on the wind acting as a summons to predatory insects, which are drawn towards the marauding pests. Ladybirds and lacewings, both voracious predators of aphids, respond in this way.

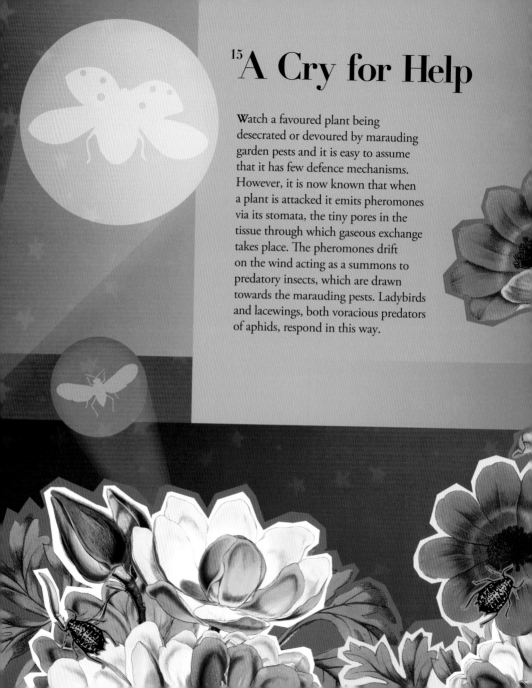

Chemical warfare does not stop there: when aphids come under attack they also release a pheromone called (E)-^{2}-farnesene (EBF), which causes other aphids to flee the predators. Plant pathologists, curious about such messaging systems are now breeding plants that relentlessly produce the aphid alarm pheromone in the hope that it might cause aphids to scatter. However, the research has demonstrated that the aphids instead of fleeing seem to become 'deaf' to the pheromone signals. Unphased, scientists now believe that the same systems can permanently attract predators to the plants, providing an entrenched defence to attack.

This cry for help could explain why some plants of the same species are better than others at resisting pests.

Imagine a crop that was able to tell a farmer exactly what stresses it was facing. Such attributes are fast becoming a reality thanks to a more refined understanding of the hormones and pheromones released by plants into the environment.

If methyl jasmonate is present the plant has suffered a wound, typically from a pest, while methyl salicylate seems to be released in response to the ingress of disease. The messaging system and mechanism are varied as these chemicals can be retained and detected within the original plant; they can be carried on a third party, for instance the hand of a gardener when pruning; or they can drift on the wind and alert other plants of the same species of impending attack, prompting them to mobilise their defences.

The quantities released are difficult to accurately detect with the current technology, but the hope is that future refinements will make it possible to finally decode the language of plants.

In 1915 the War Office placed the following advertisement in *The Gardeners' Chronicle*, "We would be glad to know of any supplies of *Rhamnus Frangula* in this country. Estate owners who have plantations of Rhamnus and are willing to sell should communicate with the Secretary, War Office, Whitehall."

Far from indicating a sudden passion for gardening the search for this wood was motivated by experiences on the battlefield dating back to the fifteenth century, most notably the tradition of manufacturing gunpowder. Following the publication in 1785 and 1791 of research by William Congreve into different types of wood, which concluded that Alder Buckthorn, now called *Frangula alnus*, produced the finest gunpowder, a concerted effort was made to harvest this wood for the war effort.

It seems that the properties of Alder Buckthorn, and those of Willow and Alder also, make them ideal for producing a pure charcoal that burns with predictable speed and reliability.

¹⁸Smoking Gun

Nicotiana, the tobacco plant, was presented as a gift to Christopher Columbus along with other dried leaves by tribes of the New World. Unsure of its worth and purpose, he apparently disposed of the collection. With the annual worldwide death toll from tobacco-related illnesses now estimated to exceed six million there are many who must believe Columbus's initial reaction was the right one. However, after widespread introduction to Europe and Asia throughout the sixteenth and seventeenth centuries, and Sir Walter Raleigh's talent for convincing the Elizabethan court to take up smoking, a habit was formed. All early use was confined to smoking in pipes, chewing, dipping or burning within incense mixtures, with the emergence of the cigarette only occurring in 1832. Apparently all the pipes of the Egyptian artillerymen fighting in the First Egyptian-Ottoman War were damaged and they took to rolling tobacco leaves in the fuse papers from their canons. This practice spread during various military conflicts, including the Crimean War, and was eventually adopted as the preferred way to partake of tobacco.

When in 1853 Levi Strauss made canvas into miners' overalls he received many complaints that they chafed the wearers. So he used instead a twilled cotton cloth from France called 'serge de Nîmes' after the town where it was manufactured and an iconic garment was born. 'De Nîmes' was later shortened to denim.

Little did Strauss suspect the consequences of the popularisation not just of his denim jeans but also the blue dye that created such rich and vibrant hues in fabrics. Derived from Indigofera species the plants are pea relatives and were traditionally cultivated to extract dye for use in patterned fabrics and paintings. In India indigo was also used to colour paper for letters, medicine wrappings and religious writings. In the mid-nineteenth century the British planters who owned the factories that processed the indigo forced Indian farmers to cultivate it in preference to food and cash crops, duping them into taking out high-interest loans, called dadon, which ensured that many remained in debt for life as the planters paid them only 2.5% of the market price for their crop.

The farmers revolted in 1859 but quickly realised that as they had no arms passive resistance was their only form of attack. Not a single indigo seedling was planted in that year.

RC. Majumdar goes so far as to call it "a forerunner of the non-violent passive resistance later successfully adopted by Gandhi."

The links between a tropical tree
and soldiers fighting in bitterly cold
conditions in the Napoleonic Wars
may not, at first consideration, be
obvious, that is until the properties
of the tree are revealed. *Pimenta
dioica* produces a wealth of lush
green leaves on smooth grey barked
stems that also carry small white
blooms in summer. It is these that
produce what is commonly referred
to as Allspice, a seasoning that, as
its name suggests, evokes memories
of cinnamon, ginger, cloves and
nutmeg. Grind allspice into a
powder, sprinkle it liberally into
your socks and the inherent volatile
oils serve to warm the skin.

First popularised by Russian
infantrymen the practice, it is said,
not only led to more contented toes
but also to less smelly feet. It is this
side effect that is attributed to the
fashion for men's toiletries with hints
of pepper and spice.

Chives (*Allium schoenoprasum*) occupy a prominent position in folklore for their powers to ward off evil spirits. They were traditionally used in fortune telling, and hanging bunches of this onion relative in the house was a sure way of keeping diseases and disaster at bay. Chives can also be called on to fight off the effects of poisons, to aid digestion, and stimulate the circulatory system, as a diuretic and as an antiseptic.

They are also thought to provide a quick energy boost, which explains why, in a dispatch from the front line during the American Civil War, General Ulysses S. Grant, sent his famous ultimatum, "I will not move my troops until the chives arrive."

As if being in the heat of battle wasn't sufficient distraction, German soldiers during the First World War had to contend with uniforms made of Nettles (*Urtica dioica*). Cotton was in short supply so the German population collected tens of thousands of kilograms of wild Nettles for the fibre content of their stems. A close examination revealed that German uniforms contained some 85% of the plant fibre, with about 40 kilograms of Nettles required to manufacture a single shirt.

Related to Hemp the fibre had been used to create coarse textured cloth and sacking since the seventeenth century. Around the globe civilisations familiar with the Nettle created everything from fishing nets to lingerie from these invasive, inhospitable plant's. Today, there is further research into the use of Nettles for the production of textiles following concerns about the pesticides necessary for the production of cotton.

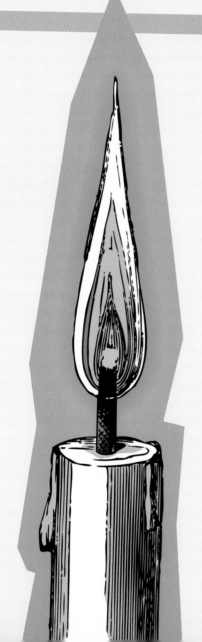

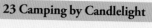
The extremes of temperature in the desert and arid landscapes of New Mexico provoke an ingenious response from some plants. *Euphorbia cerifera*, a stiffly-branched, inhospitable-looking perennial has devised the tactic of coating its leaves and most notably its stems in a thick wax, which is at its most concentrated during periods of drought and heat, preventing water loss and limiting UV damage. Noticed by early Spanish colonists in the region, the wax was harvested and used to manufacture small candles, hence the plants common name Candelilla. Interest in the plant was re-ignited during the two World Wars as the Euphorbia was once again called on to relinquish its waxy coat, this time to be applied to the canvas tents and canopies of soldiers for waterproofing.

Today the plant still provides wax, now seen most frequently in chewing gum, cosmetics and lip balms.

The ancient British game of Conkers, the art of striking one horse chestnut with another to see which is demolished first, was originally played with snails on strings. When the Horse Chestnut (*Aesculus hippocastanum*) was introduced into Western Europe from the Balkan peninsular in the mid sixteenth century the game was revolutionised but few could have predicted the further consequences of widely planting this horticultural curiosity in Britain.

Following a shortage of munitions during the First World War a secret silo was developed at Holton Heath in Dorset where thousands of tons of Horse Chestnuts, collected by schoolchildren, were used to produce acetone, which was used as a solvent in the production of cordite. Chaim Weizmann, who had emigrated from Europe in 1904, had invented a process for the production of acetone based on the bacterial fermentation of maize starch and was put in charge of the project.

When supplies of maize ran out, he replaced it with horse chestnuts. David Lloyd George was so grateful to Weizmann that when he became Prime Minister he gave him direct access to Balfour, leading to the Balfour Declaration of 1917, which stated that the British government viewed with qualified favour "the establishment in Palestine of a national home for the Jewish people." This left, in Lloyd George's words "a permanent mark on the map of the world." Chaim Weizmann went on to become the first president of Israel.

The Truth about Mandrake

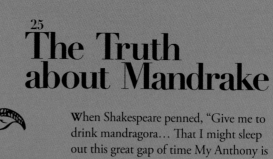

When Shakespeare penned, "Give me to drink mandragora… That I might sleep out this great gap of time My Anthony is away" in *Antony and Cleopatra* there was a clear understanding of the properties of the Mandragora, or Mandrake plant, which belongs to the nightshades family (Solanaceae). A stem-less perennial native to Italy, Turkey and Greece, the plant acquired its common name because its roots divide and fork unusually (known botanically as bifurcate), causing them to resemble the torso and limbs of a man.

MARIS

FOEMINÆ

A popular painkiller in the Middle Ages some suggest that it was offered to Christ on the cross as was the practice at the time. Folklore states that to gain access to the all-powerful roots it is necessary to carefully extract them by pulling vigorously and that the shrieks of the man may be heard as the limbs are torn off and the roots rendered useless.

These roots contain atropine, scopolamine and hyoscyamine and can lead to dramatic, debilitating effects on the user as they are hallucinogenic and hypnosis and delirium inducing. High doses can even lead to coma. These widely-documented properties may have led to twentieth-century investigations into the plant as a possible 'truth drug'.

Fight with Cakes and Jam

During the night-time bombardment of German positions in the Second World War by the RAF there was concern that targets were being missed because of poor visibility. In an effort to remedy the situation pilots were advised to eat Bilberry jam on their cakes and in their sandwiches prior to flying. Many reported remarkable results and Bilberry jam, produced from the plant *Vaccinium myrtillus*, a heathland resident, became an essential food. Some fifty years later researchers highlighted the real talents of the plant demonstrating an increase in blood supply to the eye, improved nearsightedness, and, after prolonged use, an improvement in visual acuity.

Research suggests that the anthocyanoides present in the fruit are amongst the most powerful antioxidants, with some authorities rating it higher in effectiveness than vitamins A and E for preventing free radical damage. Quite why the Bilberry has such an effect on the eye is still debated and contested. Contemporary research indicates it may also benefit patients suffering from osteoarthritis and gout.

Hanging off the cliffs and rocky crags at over 1000 metres altitude in some of the coldest regions of the northern hemisphere including the Alps, Pyrenees and Rocky Mountains, *Rhodiola rosea*, the Rose Root is a persistent and resilient plant. Related to the Sedum, its succulent grey foliage drapes over the rocks, while sulphur yellow blooms entice pollinating insects to rich nectar rewards.

In folklore the ground root was used by Russians, Siberians and Scandinavians as an energy boost, especially in harsh, cold environments. Such is the popularity of the plant that KGB agents were equipped with supplements of its extracts to improve physical and mental endurance and concentration in stressful conditions and situations. It also apparently formed part of the training diet of Soviet athletes.

Modern research demonstrates the extract is an adaptogen that helps maintain optimal metabolic equilibrium by balancing immune systems and endocrine hormones, vital during times of physical and mental stress.

42

The pride of receiving a rosette at the local Pony Club drives some to extraordinary lengths when it comes to the performance of their horse, but the Imperial Dictionary of the English Language offers a troubling insight:

"Figging...To treat a horse in such a way as to make the animal appear lively, as by putting a piece of ginger into the anus."

This was also known as 'feaguing', and it is reported that in some stables handlers who showed horses without first administering ginger were disciplined. The purpose was to allow the volatile oils to irritate the horse, causing it to prance, appear lively and restless, and to hold its tail aloft, convincing onlookers of its spritely, virile nature.

Curiously, the modern use of *Zingiber officinale* concentrates on its sedative and antibacterial properties when it is taken internally. and in the plant's remarkable ability to relieve nausea resulting from seasickness, morning sickness and chemotherapy. Ginger biscuits, root ginger and ginger in crystallised form have all proved useful.

The wonderful golden fruits of the Quince (*Cydonia oblonga*), were traditionally harvested as the leaves fell from the plant in autumn and prior to the fruits fully ripening. They were then placed in drawers with ladies' underwear until, after a few weeks, the fruits ripened. In the ripening process the fruits scented the underwear.

Ethylene, which is essential in the ripening process, is released by the growing tips of roots, flowers, damaged tissue, and ripening fruit. The hormone has multiple effects on plants, one of which is that it ensures that the starch in the fleshy part of the fruit is converted to sugar. The sweeter fruit is more attractive to animals, so they will eat it, disperse the seeds and ensure the propagation of the plant. When ethylene initiates the reaction in which the starch is converted into sugar it emits the distinctive fragrance found in the popular boiled sweets known as Pear Drops.

The essential bitter flavour in Tonic Water is derived from the bark of the Cinchona tree. Also known as the Fever Tree it is a native of Peru and Bolivia, where the native tribes used the bark extract to relax muscles and prevent shivering at low temperatures and during sickness.

It is rich in alkaloids the most potent being Quinine, a compound used to treat malaria since the 1630s. So valuable was the anti-malarial tonic during the great ages of European exploration of the tropics and sub-tropics that its trade was lucrative and disputed. By the Second World War the principal supplies of Quinine came from Asia, particularly Indonesia and the Philippines. As the war developed the Germans captured European stockpiles of the drug in Amsterdam, while Japanese troops threatened to take Asian supplies. In a desperate effort to limit their losses the Americans had stolen a reputed four million seeds from the Philippines prior to its capture.

These were shipped to the United States for germination and then on to Costa Rica for cultivation. These, combined with supplies from other parts of South America stemmed the effect of the disease amongst the Allies, although an estimated 60,000 Allied troops still died of malaria during the Asian campaign.

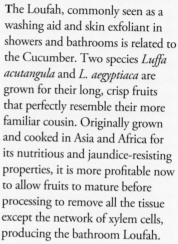

The Loufah, commonly seen as a washing aid and skin exfoliant in showers and bathrooms is related to the Cucumber. Two species *Luffa acutangula* and *L. aegyptiaca* are grown for their long, crisp fruits that perfectly resemble their more familiar cousin. Originally grown and cooked in Asia and Africa for its nutritious and jaundice-resisting properties, it is more profitable now to allow fruits to mature before processing to remove all the tissue except the network of xylem cells, producing the bathroom Loufah.

Research has recently concentrated on the apparent natural antibacterial properties of the tissue in the production of fine grade air filters.

The distinctive and popular tweeds of Scotland, famed in the clan tartans and heraldry are reliant on the most diminutive of structures, the Lichen. Neither plant nor fungus, these curious lichens are a rare example of a symbiotic relationship between fungi and photosynthetic cells, usually algae. Often seen as slow growing, complex tattoos on rocks and in woodland they yield a distinctive array of hues for use in dying. Most sought after are species from the Parmelia, Ochrolechia, and Evernia genera. It is these that provide the famous earth colours of the tweeds that completely transformed the economy of the Scottish islands and ensured the worldwide popularity of tweed.

Originally the pigments were not held well by the wool and it was necessary to fix them chemically, a process traditionally achieved by soaking the fabric in stale human urine. Undetected by many drawn to the highland fashion, the origin of the Lichen fixative became clear when the fabric got wet.

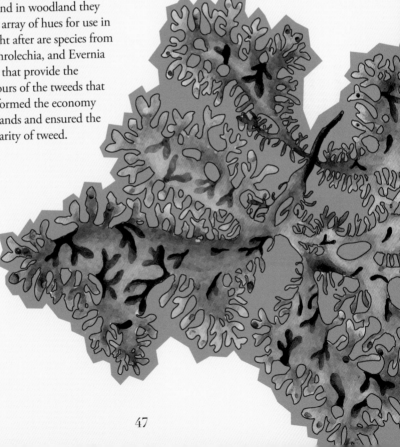

Puzzling Monkeys

Distinctive in stature, texture and habit the Monkey Puzzle tree (*Araucaria araucana*) was a curiosity when introduced to Western gardens in 1795. Heralding from the mountainous forests of central Chile it was first encountered by Westerners in the 1780s. Initially tempted by its towering, perfectly straight trunks, the Spanish unsuccessfully attempted to use the wood for repairing their ships.

Local tribes developed a taste for its nuts and it was during a banquet with the Chilean governor that explorer and naturalist Archibald Menzies was served the delicacy. Clearing his plate of the nuts he stashed a collection of them on board ship, eventually returning to Britain with five healthy seedlings.

The common English name, Monkey Puzzle, is said to derive from a conversation between the proud owner and an admirer of a tree in Pencarrow Gardens, Cornwall. They noted that the stems and branches were so barbed and prickly with savage needles that it would constitute a difficult puzzle for monkeys trying to climb it. This might have been an accurate observation if there were any monkeys native to the regions of Chile where the tree originated.

34
Grasp the Nettle

Aesop recounts the story of the boy who picked some Nettles very carefully and ran crying to his mother, who explained that he should have grasped them firmly to avoid being stung.

In many parts of Europe prior to the use of herbicides the problem facing farmers was a lack of nutritious fodder for their animals, especially in those regions where Nettle patches prospered because animals, fearful of the stings, do not graze them. However, harvesting and drying this common invasive weed eliminates the sting allowing the plant to be used as dry fodder. When it is fed to cattle the milk yield increases; chicken fed on it lay with greater enthusiasm; and horses' coats turn lustrous and full of vibrancy leading horse breeders to feed it to their animals prior to taking them to market in order to boost sales.

The habit of enhancing the lips with lipstick is found in many civilisations dating back thousands of years and is thought to relate to the male attraction to enlarged and reddened genitals of the female when most receptive.

The ancient Japanese were amongst the first to apply make-up seeking out an extract of *Carthamnus tinctorius*, a branched thistle commonly called the Safflower. It was liberally blended with waxes before application, possibly making it the first lipstick. Powdered forms were also mixed with lead powder (now known to be highly toxic) before being applied to the cheeks as rouge to contour the cheeks.

The ancient Mesopotamians were also attracted to lipstick employing dye from Mulberry and crushed semi-precious stones for a glistening effect. Meanwhile Cleopatra is said to have used crushed carmine beetles and ants.

Whoever was first to wear it may be lost in history but the first to ban it was the Catholic Church who, in Medieval Europe, suggested that red lips were the incarnation of Satan and the reserve of prostitutes.

The Gooseberry is a curious plant that until the mid-seventeenth century received little comment or notice. Derived from the currant family it originates in the cooler climes of Asia and throughout Europe where its tart berries did little to excite the palate. Fortunes altered radically though with the onset of the Black Death when the acidic fruits were hailed by many as a remedy. Consequently dishes and pies, sauces and preserves suddenly flourished with the wealthy cultivating dozens of different forms. Available in shades of white, green, purple and yellow they ranged from extended oblong to pea-like in shape.

An industry may have been stimulated but there is little evidence to support the plague claims except that the fruits are naturally high in vitamins A and C, and so are generally good for health. Neither is there any evidence to support the once held belief that fairies live under these thorny shrubs despite their alternative common name of Faeberry or Fayberry. Incidentally, this is the origin of the tale that unplanned children emerge from under the Gooseberry bush; it was the fairies who were to blame.

Derived from the Greek word for trophy, probably because of its shield-shaped leaves and helmet-shaped flowers, the Tropaeolum, or Nasturtium as it is commonly called, has aroused a flurry of interest amongst artisan chefs because its warmly hued blooms ignite the appearance of a tossed salad.

Not only do these flowers excite the eye, they also invigorate the gut. Filled with the antibiotic agent tromalyt, the effects of eating them can be detected in the urine within an hour of consumption. Passing through the intestine they have been shown to attack some harmful microorganisms, including several forms resistant to conventional antibiotic drugs. Their antibacterial and antifungal properties are said to cleanse the mouth, making them one of the finest natural toothpastes, while their peppery taste stimulates the appetite.

In the Middle Ages Nettles were applied to the head to cure baldness. Well, science now supports this theory. An extract from the root of the Nettle apparently controls Dihydrotestosterone (DHT) levels and it has been shown that an excess of DHT is linked to male pattern balding. Reduce the DHT and hair flourishes.

Devil of a Hangover

For a relatively easily grown plant with a strong flavour the common Parsley is strangely absent from historic medicine and culinary dishes, revealing a more sinister association.

The 'Devil's Herb', as Parsley is known, was one of the most feared plants to grow in any garden. In Ancient Greece and Rome it was the symbol of a glorious death. The victors at the Isthmian and Nemean Games may have been presented with a wreath of Parsley but the same Parsley was used to decorate the tombs of the dead. So feared was the plant that folklore states that a Grecian army about to do battle with a Celtic tribe fled the battlefield after a herd of asses loaded with Parsley ran through its ranks.

Reputed to travel to the Devil and back nine times before sprouting, the plant has a long germination period, a natural mechanism to prolong the colony of plants and secure favourable conditions. Some British folklore states that to protect the household only a woman should ever plant the seeds and then only when the church bells are ringing.

The Ancients may have felt the Devil was present in the plant but they were sufficiently keen to run the risk of the consequences as it was traditional to wear a crown of Parsley at feasts to prevent a hangover the following morning. Similarly they believed that chewing the seeds of the plant would provide greater tolerance to alcohol.

Curiously, a tea made from the herb, which is rich in iron, minerals and vitamins, is indeed a good cure for a hangover.

Garlic (*Allium sativum*) has undergone something of a popularity boost in recent years thanks to a wealth of research suggesting remarkable health benefits. Assisting in lowering blood pressure, reducing cholesterol levels, possessing natural antibiotic properties, a significant antioxidant effect in the case of aged garlic and even better results from black garlic are amongst the claims generally supported by science.

This had not gone unnoticed by the Ancients: they regarded a good workman as one who consumed copious quantities of the plant. In Egypt during the reign of King Tut, himself buried in a cask of garlic, a handsome male slave could be bought for fifteen pounds of garlic and the slaves who built the Pyramids had raw garlic added to their rations of bread to ward off illness and increase stamina. Anyone threatening to flee was given more garlic.

The troubled Vincent Van Gogh is perhaps not the most likely person to receive medicinal advice from but historians suggest that his doctor, Paul-Ferdinand Gachet, treated Van Gogh with Foxglove, (*Digitalis purpurea*).

Digitalin compounds extracted from the leaf have been shown to affect the heart, most notably those called cardiac glycosides that stimulate a strengthening of the heartbeat and the control of irregular heart rhythms. First noted by William Withering in 1785, while supposedly observing a local herbalist consume the potion, Digitalins now support heart surgery.

Unfortunately for Van Gogh it was unlikely that his heart was the problem, as many suggest his symptoms align with epilepsy for which the Digitalin would have offered only a sedative effect. One possible side effect of consuming the drug is the adjustment of colour differentiation, which may have led Van Gogh to paint many of his works in yellow hues.

The prospect of a plant foraging around for a specific host before using specially adjusted cells to pierce the host tissue and suck life from it is reminiscent of adaptations that Triffids might make, and certainly not an activity that we might expect in our gardens.

Much research has been conducted into the chemical signals plants emit and the effects of these on other organisms but one startling piece of research indicates that the British and European native *Cuscuta europaea*, or Dodder is advanced in the deployment of such tactics.

Capable of existing on a wide variety of host plants, this apparently leafless, parasitic vine-like plant appears to cast seed that, while in the seedling stage, is equipped to read the chemical signals emitted by nearby plants. Even more startling is its ability to then create a hierarchy of desirable hosts, before growing in the direction of the most nutritionally suitable plant to bleed dry.

Such science brings into question the motives of the individuals in the folk tale: "A girl having plucked a vine, with the thought of the young man in mind tossed the vine over her shoulder, into the weeds of host species of this Dodder [...]. The second day after she would return to see whether the Dodder had attached itself and was growing on the host. If so, she went away content with full assurance of her lover's sincerity and faithfulness."

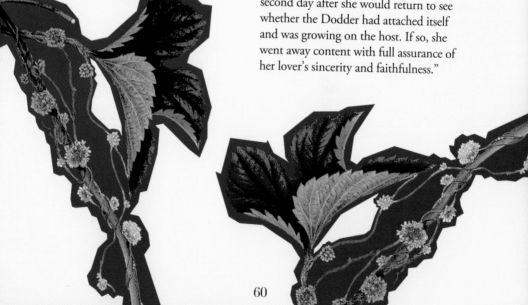

PT 109 was the motor torpedo boat commanded by a young John F. Kennedy on 2nd August 1943 when it was attacked off the Solomon Islands by a Japanese destroyer. Following an explosion the survivors swam to a nearby island and lived on a diet of Coconuts and fresh water.

Known to be nutritionally superior as a food the flesh, milk and water are all beneficial while the oil is of special interest because it possesses healing properties far beyond that of any other dietary oil and has long been extensively used by Asian and Pacific populations.

More than providing sustenance for the shipwrecked American seamen for almost a week, the Coconut, so called because the Spanish thought the three spots on the husk resembled the face of a monkey or coco, was to be their salvation.

Following the explosion a lookout on a neighbouring island despatched two locals in a dug-out canoe to the island thought to be closest to where the boat was sunk. There they found Kennedy and his crew but speaking no English, and not having

a canoe large enough for rescue were unsure of the next step. Apparently Kennedy scratched a message on the husk of a Coconut that read "NAURO ISL... COMMANDER... NATIVE KNOWS POS'IT...HE CAN PILOT... 11 ALIVE..NEED SMALL BOAT... KENNEDY." The two natives then headed 35 miles through enemy waters in the dug-out canoe to deliver the Coconut to the Allies. Kennedy is said to have kept the Coconut and placed it on his desk in the Oval Office.

Shen Nung, who lived around 2695 BC, is considered the Father of Chinese medicine. It is recorded that he tasted 365 herbs, many toxic or previously unknown, before writing his discourse *On Herbal Medical Experiment Poisons*.

One story tells of his search for eternal life and how he dispatched twenty-four children on a dangerous journey to a faraway island. It was said that on the island grew a rare flower that would bestow eternal life if picked by children. What the children found when they arrived at the island were golden Chrysanthemums.

The result was the Chinese reverence for the Chrysanthemum and the use of Chrysanthemums in teas. Modern analysis indicates that such brews contain vitamins A and B1, glycosides, amino acids, and beneficial flavonoids. The drink is said to have an inhibiting effect on bacteria, to have antiviral properties while enhancing capillary resistance, and to help cure high blood pressure, heart colic, coronary heart disease, arteriosclerosis and high cholesterol, to relieve congestion, palpitation, short breath, dizziness, migraine headaches, colds, flu, and the list goes on! But it is worth noting that, ironically, although Shen Nung consumed great quantities of it, he died of a toxic overdose. However, Chrysanthemum tea is still drunk and used in Chinese medicine today.

The health benefits of vitamin C have long been appreciated but during the Second World War its availability was hindered by limited fruit and vegetable imports. Undeterred, the British Government enlisted the help of a drinks company called Carters. The aim was to manufacture a vitamin-rich syrup for widespread free distribution. The plant that was chosen for the purpose was perfect for cultivation in the cool, maritime climate of the British Isles, the Blackcurrant. And so Ribena was born.

By contrast, the Blackcurrant was banned from cultivation in the United States because it was thought to carry the disease 'white pine blister' that could devastate forests. This ban remained in place in some States until 2006.

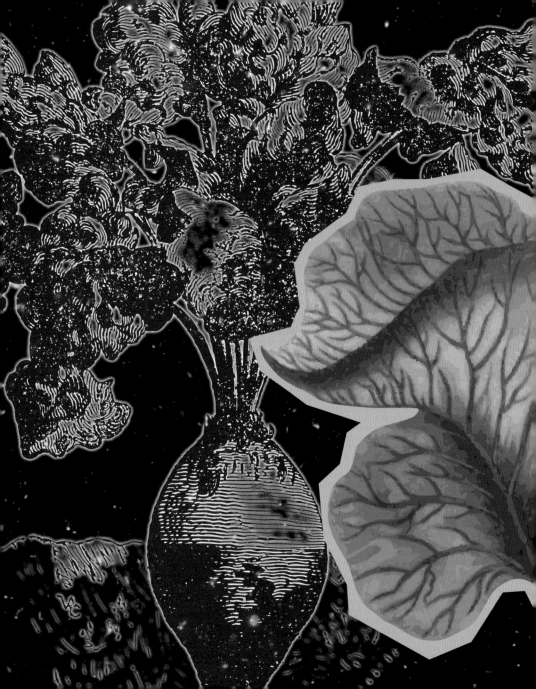

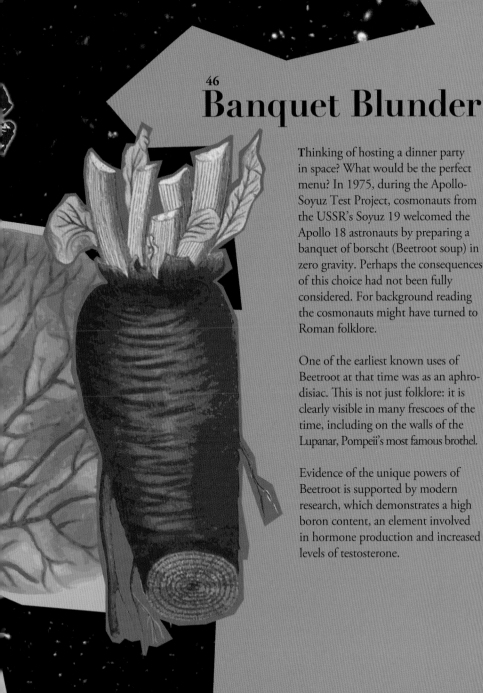

Banquet Blunder

Thinking of hosting a dinner party in space? What would be the perfect menu? In 1975, during the Apollo-Soyuz Test Project, cosmonauts from the USSR's Soyuz 19 welcomed the Apollo 18 astronauts by preparing a banquet of borscht (Beetroot soup) in zero gravity. Perhaps the consequences of this choice had not been fully considered. For background reading the cosmonauts might have turned to Roman folklore.

One of the earliest known uses of Beetroot at that time was as an aphrodisiac. This is not just folklore: it is clearly visible in many frescoes of the time, including on the walls of the Lupanar, Pompeii's most famous brothel.

Evidence of the unique powers of Beetroot is supported by modern research, which demonstrates a high boron content, an element involved in hormone production and increased levels of testosterone.

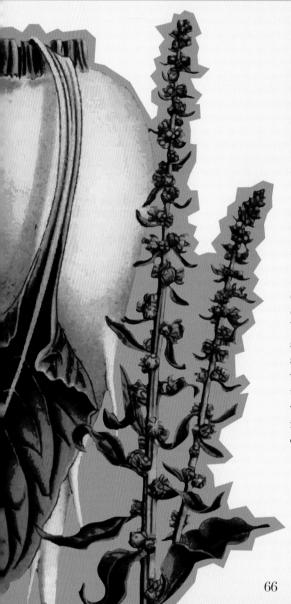

Beetroot, like Chard and Sugar Beet, is part of the large Amaranth family, all of which use their large swollen roots to store energy reserves in the form of carbohydrates. Carbohydrates can easily be converted into simple sugars to provide energy which assists the plants' growth and flowering. This wasn't overlooked by Frenchman Benjamin Delessert who, in 1812, devised a method of extracting the sugar on an industrial scale for human consumption. So successful was his process that by the mid 1830s France was the largest sugar producer from beet in the world.

Delessert's work was fuelled by a desire to rid France of the friction and conflict in the sugarcane fields of the Western Colonies. His success broke the stranglehold of sugar cane in the world supply of sugar, weakening the political will of Western governments to support the slave trade, which until that time was estimated to have been responsible for millions of people from the African continent being sold into slavery.

The eternal harbinger of spring immortalised in William Wordsworth's poetry, the Daffodil possesses a charm and character that warms the heart on the most boisterous of spring days. The history is less optimistic in outlook. The Daffodil, or Narcissus, is named after Narkissos, a beautiful youth from Greek mythology who, on seeing his own reflection in a pool, became mesmerised by its beauty. Besotted with himself he eventually died numb with sleep and was turned into the Daffodil.

Its introduction to northern Europe was no less dramatic. According to folklore a Crusader impressed by the diversity and beauty of the plants during his religious travels in southern Europe and the Middle East, dispatched some bulbs to his sweetheart. On his return, the bulbs were presented at a feast organised for the lovers. Unfortunately for the intrepid Crusader his lover lacked culinary skills and mistook the Daffodil bulbs for Onions. They both died of alkaloid poisoning, specifically lycorine. Mammals are wiser and don't graze daffodils.

The Perfect Cut

When it came to inventions Victorian Britons generally were not shy, except for Edwin Beard Budding. In 1830 he worked in a mill in the Gloucestershire valleys, preparing cloths. While observing the way in which the rotating blades of machinery cut the threads of the cloth Budding allowed his mind to wander.

He secretly, quietly and under cover of darkness recreated the same rotating blades on a hand-powered machine. His stealth owed little to a fear of industrial espionage and more to the fact that his fellow millworkers thought his proposals ridiculous. Finally Budding perfected his invention: it was only 19 inches wide and he called it the lawn mower, which was to transform British lawns and the concept of cultivating grass in the garden.

Until Budding's invention cutting grass involved teams of men scything the grass sward, an awkward operation that relied on skill and practice. With standard length tools each man of a different height inevitably cut the grass at different lengths; to correct this each wore wooden clogs of a prescribed height to adjust the height of his cut. With Budding's invention out went labour-intensive teams, rough cuts and any similarity to a meadow; in came the British obsession with stripes and perfect lawns.

During the Victorian obsession with recording all manner of diversity in the natural world, no matter how small or trivial, there was a special interest in the meaning of flowers. Known broadly as the Language of Flowers it attributed signals, symbolism or messaging to every bloom. In this way, it is said, conversations could be sustained without the utterance of words. Fragments of this language remain in our culture today but some are forgotten at our peril.

Send a Bluebell for humility; Pink Camellia to say 'I long for you'; a red carnation to announce 'my heart aches for you'; Hibiscus talks of your lover's beauty; Ivy states eternal affection; and the Lily confirms purity.

Select your blooms carefully though: a yellow Carnation says 'you disappoint me'; Meadowsweet means uselessness; and a yellow rose, seen at so many weddings, confirms 'I have been unfaithful'.

51 Holly Spirit

The common Holly (*Ilex aquifolium*) was a plant revered in pre-Christian times as a home to fairies. Throughout Europe Holly was believed to ward off evil and protect the house from disaster, but by the Middle Ages it had assumed an entirely different function: there emerged a belief that drinking ale under a Holly would allow copious consumption without fear of a hangover or drunkenness. It is for this reason that so many public houses, taverns and bars in Britain carry Holly in their name.

Moss saves Lives on the Battlefield

Sphagnum Moss, a common inhabitant of woodland, moor land and acidic damp soils throughout the northern temperate regions evolved around 350 million years ago as a simple plant with little cellular distinction in its overall structure. All the more remarkable then that this lowly species, which populated the globe before dinosaurs, reptiles and flying insects, went on to save thousands of lives in the twentieth century.

In common with many discoveries, the tremendous potential of moss initially – and again in more recent times – occurred by accident, or rather as the result of an accident. In 1882, deep in the Bavarian forests a logging accident led a forester to reach for some sphagnum moss in a desperate attempt to stem the bleeding from his arm. Doctors who treated the patient subsequently were astounded by the unusual cleanliness and rapid healing of the wound. In 1900 Scottish doctor Charles Cathcart was translating medical files from Germany when he found a reference to the mysterious healing properties of the moss. Intrigued he set about conducting numerous trials, which revealed that the huge absorbency properties of Sphagnum Moss – it can absorb seven times its own weight in liquid – helped keep wounds dry.

As a result Cathcart set about testing field dressings made from moss, collecting, drying and cleaning the raw material before soaking it and then finally applying it to the wound. So impressed was he with the results that he penned an article to the Director General, Army Medical Services on 5th January 1916 in which he extolled the virtues of this compressed and therefore space-saving product, its ease of manufacture compared with available alternatives, and the simplicity of application. So convincing was Cathcart's case that the practice was adopted and the children of Britain were mobilised by a War Office campaign to collect wild moss from the countryside. They even had special permission to collect it on Sundays.

The efficacy of the sphagnum-moss-based dressings was never officially recorded but there was a later acknowledgment from the Army that without the moss dressings the already high death tolls would have spiralled from unstemmed bleeding and infected wounds.

Perhaps what Cathcart didn't identify was that this simple plant had served a similar purpose for generations. Some evidence exists of its use in the Crimean War and in domestic situations in Germany. Even at the battle of Flodden, fought on 9th September 1513 between the invading Scots army under King James IV and an English army commanded by Thomas Howard, Earl of Surrey, moss was said to be used to stem bleeding. Recognised as the largest battle between the two fractious nations it eventually ended in victory for the English. More recently archaeological excavations of Bronze Age burials in Scotland revealed wounds packed with moss suggesting Cathcart's observations are more rediscovery than pioneering work.

Cathcart's trials revealed the value of the product's absorbency and cleanliness but he opted to advise sterilisation of the moss as he was uncertain of its microbial content. Modern analysis indicates that most samples are free of problematic organisms. It is in fact rich in Penicillium, a soil fungus which, like Sphagnum Moss flourishes in cool, moist climates. Charles Cathcart was perhaps tantalisingly close to pre-empting Alexander Fleming's 1929 discovery of the Penicillium genus and its use in controlling bacteria.

A Forgotten Tree

Imagine walking under the canopy of a tree known to be 200 million years old, a plant that has remained unchanged and unadulterated since Tyrannosaurus roamed past, Triceratops grazed nearby and Pterosaurs flew overhead. This was a time when flowering plants and their pollinating insects emerged and populated a planet of tropical seas and tempestuous plate tectonics; *Gingko biloba*, the Maidenhair Tree is such a specimen.

Commonly found in parks and gardens, it is the only remaining member of its genus, which is the only remaining genus in its family, which is the only remaining family in its order, which is the only remaining order in its class. Put bluntly this is not only a living fossil but a unique living fossil tree and botanically a key link between the evolutionary groups of lower plants, the mosses and ferns, and the higher plants, conifers and flowering plants.

As peculiar in appearance as it is in history, it is a broad leaved, deciduous cone-producing tree, the only one remaining. Reaching 40 metres or so in height and with fan-shaped leaves it carries male and female flowers on separate plants.

Quite how this tree, and no other from such distant times remains intact has puzzled botanists, but it shows remarkable resilience to severe climatic alteration and chokingly high levels of pollution, making it something of a cockroach of the plant kingdom.

Once common around the emerging continents it is now confined to small regions of China. Listed today by the International Union for Conservation of Nature on a red list (highly endangered), the number of Gingkos left in the wild is uncertain.

It is held as a sacred tree in both China and Japan; it is said that Confucius recited his texts from under its canopy. It has also long been part of the herbal medicine of these two ancient nations, earning a reputation for focussing the mind and alerting the senses. Modern science has explored the compounds of the plant, identifying the existence of ginkgoflavonglycoside in concentrated forms in the leaves just prior to autumn leaf fall. According to the ancient wisdom of prescribing these parts of the tree to patients the symptoms addressed by gingko extracts include short-term memory loss, dementia, depression, poor circulation, tinnitus, multiple sclerosis, depression, neuralgia and impotence. An impressive list of ailments treated thanks to the effect of the flavone glycoside, which massively increases circulation tissues, improves blood flow and in addition reduces many of the symptoms of ageing centred on memory loss and memory malfunction.

⁵⁴Angel's Trumpets and cavorting Victorian Ladies

Polite, chattering, retiring and gentle sipping of choice teas may be the impression frequently peddled of English Victorian ladies socialising in their exotic plant-filled conservatories, but it appears that this is far from the truth. Widely cultured, experienced in the intrepid tales of the Empire and vast consumers of exotica in all forms Victorian society was enriched by concepts and practices lifted and adulterated from around the world. Homes of the wealthy overflowed with goods, mementos and decoration from previously uncharted lands. Amongst such must-have riches were many plants, carefully cultivated and housed in extravagant, elaborate glazed structures, only possible because invention and industrial processes were marching ahead of exploration.

Key amongst these plant species was the Angel's Trumpet (Datura), an aptly named floral beauty generously carrying a heavenly host of pendant trumpets 30cm or more in length. Each flower has elongated stamens at the base of which, tucked deep in the flower, nectaries weep the sugar rich solution that attracts Hawkmoths, its natural pollinator, in the arid landscapes of south-west and Central America. Its intensely lemony fragrance drifts from the plant like few others. It is no surprise that each bloom has only a modest life, working hard to attract a pollinator during the few brief hours of darkness, then fading in the mid-day sun. Mirroring the frenetic activities of the Hawkmoth, Victorian society was drawn to the plant, often exhibiting it close to secluded seating, around tea tables, perhaps to appreciate the horticultural perfumery but more often to partake of the plant's darker side.

Quite what the Victorian ladies were up to is explained by the pottery patterns on utensils of native tribes in what is now New Mexico. 'Datura Man' occurs frequently in pre-colonial art; wild-faced, possessed, his body shaped like a Datura seedpod, he is a shamanic representation. In tribal rituals, the nectar, sap, leaves, stems and roots were employed in the concoction of drugs, wildly hallucinogenic potions, and teas.

The Datura is full of tropane alkaloids, primarily atropine, hyoscyamine and most frequently scopolamine; all

produce effects more pronounced than LSD, corrupting the mind with hallucinations prior to sleep. This potent and highly dangerous toxin can lead to permanent psychosis and even death following ill-informed use.

Prepared to assume the risk, the Victorian ladies politely placed their tea cups under the drooping blooms where they awaited the nectar toxins prior to polite sipping.

Such brazen indulgence in drugs may not sit comfortably with portrayals of the period but drug use and abuse was widespread at the time as were its products. Boots and Harrods both sold opium gels and laudanum, the latter being frequently prescribed to combat ailments from headaches to tuberculosis, while the former was sold openly until the British Government attributed ill-discipline in the trenches of the First World War to its mass consumption.

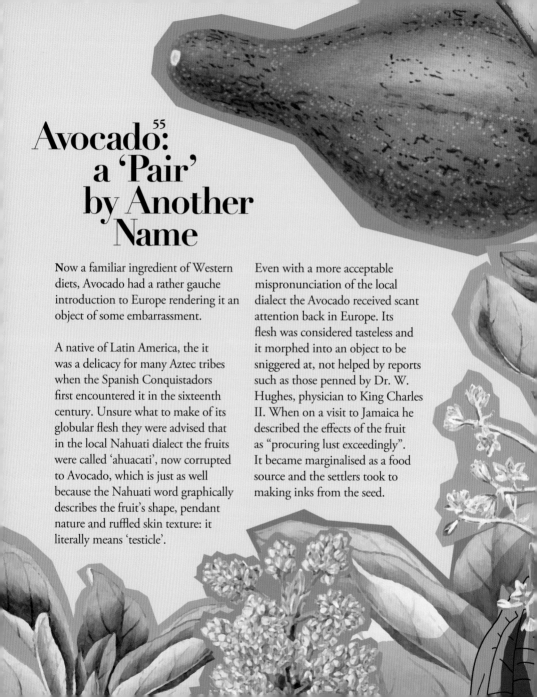

Avocado:[55] a 'Pair' by Another Name

Now a familiar ingredient of Western diets, Avocado had a rather gauche introduction to Europe rendering it an object of some embarrassment.

A native of Latin America, the it was a delicacy for many Aztec tribes when the Spanish Conquistadors first encountered it in the sixteenth century. Unsure what to make of its globular flesh they were advised that in the local Nahuati dialect the fruits were called 'ahuacati', now corrupted to Avocado, which is just as well because the Nahuati word graphically describes the fruit's shape, pendant nature and ruffled skin texture: it literally means 'testicle'.

Even with a more acceptable mispronunciation of the local dialect the Avocado received scant attention back in Europe. Its flesh was considered tasteless and it morphed into an object to be sniggered at, not helped by reports such as those penned by Dr. W. Hughes, physician to King Charles II. When on a visit to Jamaica he described the effects of the fruit as "procuring lust exceedingly". It became marginalised as a food source and the settlers took to making inks from the seed.

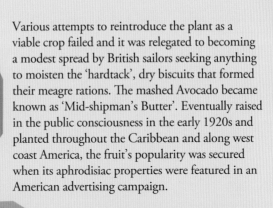

Various attempts to reintroduce the plant as a viable crop failed and it was relegated to becoming a modest spread by British sailors seeking anything to moisten the 'hardtack', dry biscuits that formed their meagre rations. The mashed Avocado became known as 'Mid-shipman's Butter'. Eventually raised in the public consciousness in the early 1920s and planted throughout the Caribbean and along west coast America, the fruit's popularity was secured when its aphrodisiac properties were featured in an American advertising campaign.

Slow to adopt the fruit so loved by the Aztecs, Western science now endorses its consumption. Avocados contain 'good' unsaturated fats that do not raise blood cholesterol. Although they are high in fat, 60% of it is monounsaturated, 20% polyunsaturated, and 20% saturated. An Avocado contains more potassium than a banana and more beta carotene than any other fruit. It is also low in sugars, curiously losing sugars as it matures rather than gaining them as in most other fruits. It contains more protein, magnesium, folic acid, thiamin, riboflavin, niacin, biotin, pantothenic acid, vitamin E, and vitamin K by weight than any other fruit. Recently, two other beneficial compounds have been identified in its flesh: beta-sitosterol and glutathione. The former promotes lower cholesterol levels and is four times more concentrated in the Avocado than in any other fruit, while glutathione is linked to a decreased risk of oral and pharyngeal cancer.

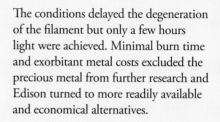

Acknowledged as one of the greatest challenges of the nineteenth century the invention of the light bulb is often attributed to Thomas Edison. In truth he was only improving on a fifty-year-old idea but his year of research could have come to nothing without plants.

In his laboratory in New Jersey between 1870 and 1880 Edison and his team researched the idea of passing electricity through a fine filament of platinum held in a vacuum within a glass bulb.

The conditions delayed the degeneration of the filament but only a few hours light were achieved. Minimal burn time and exorbitant metal costs excluded the precious metal from further research and Edison turned to more readily available and economical alternatives.

Cutting and trimming local vegetation, he carbonised filaments to test the viability of woods. Box, Hickory, Bay and Flax were amongst his early trials. Enlisting the assistance of botanists around the world he received parcels of exotic specimens. By his own admission he "tested no fewer than 6,000 vegetable growths, and ransacked the world for the most suitable filament material."

One plant he received was the bamboo, whose carbonised filament provided the eureka moment. Edison then improved burn times further with another plant, cotton, eventually producing a 16 watt bulb that burned for over 1,500 hours.

Rather than refining an idea Edison went on to revolutionise the world with electric generators, wires, cables and lamps, switches and even appliances.

Native to heavy wet soils in northern Europe the Butterbur, *Petasites hybridus*, is a vigorously spreading herbaceous species happy to colonise the banks of streams and ditches. Most identifiable are its fleshy, dinner-plate-size leaves that emerge from wet soils in late spring. To most it is an unremarkable plant, perceived more as a weed than a beautiful plant but historically it served as an ice box.

Its predisposition for watersides and large flexible leaves made it an ideal candidate for wrapping for foodstuffs. Butters, cheeses and some meats were routinely enveloped in layers of the harvested foliage before being submerged in the water. Held in place by a suitably sized rock the horticultural wrapping combined with the chill of the watercourse to refrigerate food.

But this plant offers more than housekeeping skills since it has long been associated with pain relief. Greek physicians employed chopped leaves for skin irritations, burns and boils. Carrying the seeds in bandages next to the navel apparently removed dysentery and when combined with Horseradish and Dandelion it tempered headaches.

Recent research has shown that the active substances in Butterbur are sesquiterpenes like petasin and isopetasin, and when an extract of the roots was prepared and taken for a period of three months an average 50% reduction in migraines was reported by patients. The principal downside is described as increased burping!

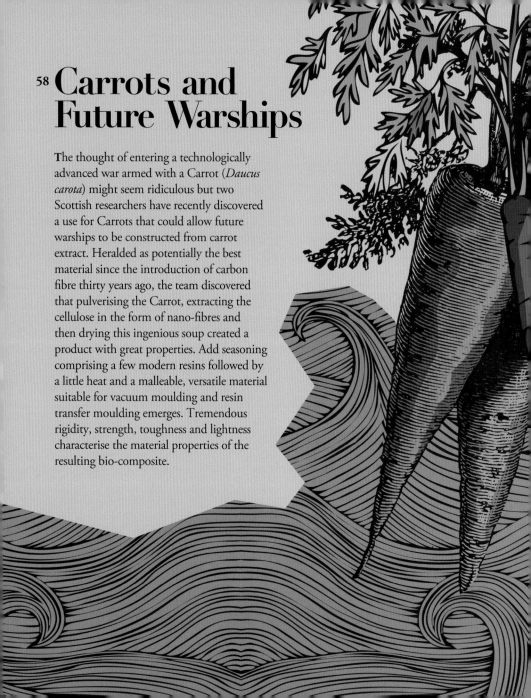

Carrots and Future Warships

The thought of entering a technologically advanced war armed with a Carrot (*Daucus carota*) might seem ridiculous but two Scottish researchers have recently discovered a use for Carrots that could allow future warships to be constructed from carrot extract. Heralded as potentially the best material since the introduction of carbon fibre thirty years ago, the team discovered that pulverising the Carrot, extracting the cellulose in the form of nano-fibres and then drying this ingenious soup created a product with great properties. Add seasoning comprising a few modern resins followed by a little heat and a malleable, versatile material suitable for vacuum moulding and resin transfer moulding emerges. Tremendous rigidity, strength, toughness and lightness characterise the material properties of the resulting bio-composite.

Quite what the humble Carrot provides that others cannot is simple: it is cheap and readily available. Research is now focussing on other fibre-rich root crops with Swedes, Turnips and Parsnips all showing promising results. The technology has already been applied to the manufacture of fly fishing rods. Currently on sale, rods are composed of about 2kg of carrot that constitute over 50% of the total material used in the production of a single rod. Key to the engineering and mechanical properties is the quality of the randomly arranged fibres. Snowboards, skateboards, bicycles, car bodies and dinghies are all planned with the aim of increasing the plant content to around 80%. Battleships could be next.

Castor Oil and the KGB

During the cold war the KGB developed a particular passion for the Castor Oil plant, (*Ricinus communis*). A statuesque and exotic plant heralding from India it is grown as a decorative annual in Northern European gardens and as a perennial in warmer climes. This relative of the Euphorbia is famed for the purgative effects of its oil, a product extracted from the seeds, sometimes called beans, and has been prescribed to patients since the Medieval period under the loose title Palma Christi or 'Hand of Christ' thanks to its cure-all properties. From acne to gout, warts to intestinal cramps and hair loss to child birth, there was nothing Castor Oil could not cure whether ingested or applied externally.

It is used today in soaps, candles, cosmetics, lubricating oils, fuels, leather preservatives, and even in the food industry to provide nutty and buttery flavours. In medicine it is used to relieve gall bladder and liver ailments, eliminate kidney infection, aid in killing off parasites and many more uses, including rapid healing of infection as it is ideal for gentle, deep-seated organ and gland cleansing. The working ingredients of this oil are ricinoleic acid, and undecylenic acid, small molecules that pass easily through the skin membrane.

Perhaps surprisingly the known toxicity of this common plant is rarely mentioned. Waste products (or mash) from the Castor Oil production process, when refined and chromatographically extracted release ricin, claimed to be one of the most deadly natural toxins. It is for this reason that the KGB, the national security agency of Russia until 1991, grew it. It is more toxic and lethal than nerve gas: as little as 500 micrograms of ricin, about the size of a pin head, could be enough to kill an adult.

So effective is it that in September 1978 it was used to assassinate the dissident Bulgarian writer and journalist Georgi Markov, who was living in exile in London. He had been the target of two failed attempts on his life but it is said that the Bulgarian secret police enlisted the help of the KGB for a third attempt. Walking to work at the BBC Markov experienced a pain like an insect bite on the back of his thigh. Within three days he was dead. Later the KGB admitted their agents had assisted the Bulgarians via a specially modified umbrella designed to pierce the skin with a microscopic needle containing a grain of ricin. Strangely, it was rumoured that there was a plan to remove the Pope using the same process, although this has never been confirmed.

60 Crazy Apple Toothpaste

Introduced to the world from India the Aubergine (*Solanum melongena*) received mixed reactions as it travelled the globe accompanying explorers and settlers. From the fifth century it was recorded in China, and was probably introduced to the West by Arabian traders. Sicily was one of the first places in Europe where it was cultivated. The first clear reference to it dates from 1309. It was called a 'melingiana' and grown in gardens along with Cucumbers and other exotic fruits.

Used in some Arab cultures as a sign of maturity it is said that a girl worthy of marriage should be able to demonstrate a hundred ways in which to prepare the fruit.

A relative of the Tomato, Tobacco and Potato, the Aubergine appears to have benefited from several facelifts since early references indicate a small pea-sized fruit of intense black colour and with an incredibly bitter taste. This should not come as a surprise as many plants of the Nightshade family, to which the Aubergine belongs, are famed for their fruits of waxy lustre and sinister poisons. In some examples, particularly the wild forms, the alkaloid rich tissue is known to cause stomach cramps, vomiting, hallucinations and even death. However, continued breeding has removed such undesirable effects from today's Aubergines. It is perhaps understandable that before such progress the Italian and Greek names for the fruit were derived from the Latin 'Mala insana' or Crazy Apple.

Gaze sufficiently far back in history and there is a clear indication that perhaps the plant was not intended for eating. According to a fifth century Chinese scroll, the Aubergine was used exclusively to make a dye from its deep purple skin. Mixed into a paste this was painted onto the teeth of fashionable women to ensure a black smile, apparently a sign that a woman was ready for marriage.

If that is not sufficient to provoke hesitation when you next contemplate a moussaka, remember the name is derived from the Persian *badingen*, the Arabic *al-badinjam* and the Spanish *albadingena*, all taken originally from a Sanskrit word, which literally translated means 'fruit of many winds', a helpful description of the side effects if consumed.

A glut of root vegetables and a need to conceal the tactically advantageous invention of radar during the summer of 1940 resulted in the popular belief that the consumption of Carrots afforded special night vision. Robert Watson Watt was requested in 1935 by the Air Ministry to create a 'Death Ray' from radio waves and discovered that radio waves bounced off objects and as a result both ground and airborne radar were developed into an effective military system. Curiously the research stations where he worked sat within the prime Carrot-growing area of the United Kingdom.

Acknowledged as a significant aid and turning point in the battle for the skies the Ministry propaganda machine swung into action with major campaigns advocating the benefits of growing and eating Carrots on health grounds and specifically to improve eyesight. Great propaganda but this was nothing new, the concept of this colourful root vegetable aiding sight can be traced back to the Middle Ages when it was considered a universal remedy for anything from snake bites and failing eyes to sexual dysfunction.

Although Carrots do contain essential Vitamin A and minerals that promote healthy eyes, post-war doctors revealed that perhaps Carrots were not the instantaneous miracle that was claimed at the time. However, recent studies do show that those who consume lutein and beta-carotene, both abundant in raw Carrots, are less likely to develop age-related eye problems such as cataracts and macular degeneration.

The multi-million dollar perfume industry launches an estimated 800 new fragrances annually. Whatever your choice of deodorant, perfume or aftershave the success of the industry and scent of its products largely depends on one plant type, the humble and largely inconspicuous Lichen.

Growing throughout the northern hemisphere on the moist bark of trees a modest Lichen, commonly known as Tree Moss, *Pseudevernia furfuracea*, is responsible for the base of almost all modern scents.

After harvesting, a technique involving the cooking of Lichen in large vats allows the draining of wax known as 'concrete' releasing the volatile oils that, depending on the tree on which it was growing, have an odour described as sharp, sweet, woody, and even tar like. It is these oils that are then blended with other more floral tones to create perfume, but essentially it is the Lichen oil that fixes or binds the scent, allowing it to linger and persist once applied.

So complex are the extracts that many are still being recorded. Recent research shows over ninety constituents in Tree Moss including depsides, depsidones and triterpenes; the latter is a complex compound that forms the building blocks of steroids, while the former are phenol compounds now being linked with antibiotic, anti-oxidant and anti-HIV properties.

Dahlia and Chips

Rivalries between the Spanish and French courts in the late 1700s almost transformed the British national dish – fish and chips. Introduced to Madrid in 1780 from Mexico, the Dahlia, now amongst the most popular of garden flowers, was grown as a potential food source thought capable of rivalling the potato, which had been introduced a few decades earlier. Championed by the Spanish after their conquests in the highlands of Mexico from the early 1500s an appetite grew to learn more of the exotic species concealed in Mexico. By 1552 Martinus de la Cruz, a student at the Spanish run College of Santa Cruz penned a medicinal text titled *An Aztec Herbal*. This eventually found its way to Spain and sparked tremendous interest at the Royal Court. King Phillip II of Spain heard rumours of great horticultural riches and despatched Hernández in 1570 on a five-year mission to document the plants and plot the region. Curiously the very text that stimulated such a passion for the flora of Mexico was lost until 1932, when it was rediscovered in the dusty vaults of the Vatican.

Daunted by the task at hand Hernández apparently spent much of his time in and around some of the most royal gardens of Mexico including Hauxtepec, the favoured garden of the captured Aztec Emperor Montezuma. Described as being six miles in circumference with many small gardens devoted to specific functions such as fragrance, fruit, vegetables and medicinal, it epitomised the sophisticated approach of the Aztecs.

From all over the Aztec empire plants were collected and cultivated on this site and many others like it, each new arrival being carefully planted in a ceremony involving the sacrifice of an animal, after which its blood and blood from the ear of a priest were used as a horticultural tonic to aid the plants' establishment, foreshadowing the current horticultural practice of applying blood and bone as a fertiliser.

After seven years Hernandez returned to Spain with over sixteen volumes of notes and drawings in which he described the Dahlia, at that time referred to locally as 'cocoxochitl', meaning 'hollow stem flower', or 'cane flower' and 'acocotli' the 'water cane', a reference to the hollow shoots of this towering Mexican wildflower. Despite his diligent efforts Hernández never got to see his work published as he died in 1578 at a time when physical specimens of the prized Dahlia plant had yet to make it across the Atlantic to Europe.

Enthusiasm for the plant was again sparked in 1789 when seeds were received in a consignment for the Madrid Royal Botanic Gardens. Antonio José Cavanilles despatched batches of the seeds to Edinburgh, Brussels, Copenhagen, Paris, London and Berlin giving rise to a great dilemma. These early seeds were species types, lacking the glamour, double flowering and extravagant colourways of the Dahlia cultivated in Mexico. The modest flowering forms divided opinion on quite how they would be best deployed as there were reports of Aztec banquets serving the tuber. which led to experiments in consumption.

The Spanish opted for cultivation of the Dahlia as an edible but in France, where the potato was popularly eaten, great scepticism existed towards the Dahlia as a food crop. Despite an initial flurry of interest the Dahlia, which actually smells and tastes more like a Parsnip than a Potato, failed to titillate the taste buds of the Continent and the Spanish conceded defeat. Several recipes persist today including Dahlia bread, Dahlia soup and fried Dahlia, all remarkably sweet on the tastebuds.

Despite being shunned by the culinary aficionados of Europe recent research proves that the Dahlia is indeed more nutritious than its rival, particularly in inulin, an essential dietary fibre that stimulates beneficial bacteria in the gut. It is considered especially helpful in the treatment of diabetes as normal digestion fails to break down the inulin into simple sugars and prevent raised blood sugar levels.

If the courts of Europe had been sufficiently convinced to favour the Dahlia rather than the Potato, the most significant historic significance of the Dahlia could have been the avoidance of the Great Irish Potato famine of the mid 1800s and the subsequent deaths or mass emigration of 25% of that nation's population.

However, having failed historically to capture the imagination of commercial crop growers and culinary aficionados the Dahlia just might be about to have its day.

Scientists were alerted to the properties of inulin in the digestion as a result of the propensity for diners to experience gassy after effects. This is simply due to the fact that only bacteria in the colon can successfully metabolise the fibre resulting in high concentrations of hydrogen and methane, embarrassing for diners but exciting for researchers seeking rocket fuel as nonhydrolised inulin can be easily converted into ethanol, a bio fuel.

Fighting Ageing by Invading

Deluged with marketing spiel concerning the latest beneficial ingredients contained in cosmetics it is worth noting that 21st century adverts are essentially peddling the same message as a document thought to date back to 1550 BC. The Ebers Papyrus is a 20 metre long scroll believed to be a condensed version of previous writings. Purchased in 1873, it suggests twelve uses for the succulent *Aloe vera* including the curing of worms, headaches, chest pains, burns, ulcers, skin diseases and allergies.

A glaucous succulent from southern and central Africa the cactus-like barbs and thick fleshy foliage suggest a plant of tempestuous nature but it has been universally known as 'miracle plant', 'medicine plant' and 'wand of heaven'. Gaining credit around the world it accompanies all great movements of peoples, repeatedly occurring in medicinal, herbal and pharmaceutical texts.

Curiously, modern medicine is less willing to embrace the plant's alleged talents despite the presence of various known beneficial ingredients such as mucopolysaccharides, which bind moisture to the skin; amino acids that soften the skin; zinc that assists in tightening pores and in the collective effect of stimulating fibroblast cells and the connective tissue, and is beneficial in reducing the ageing of skin, and in healing wounds.

Marketing claims may be considered unreasonably outlandish today but ambitious testaments have always accompanied this plant. Cleopatra, a ruler known for her intoxicating beauty and captivating sex appeal was an early devotee of *Aloe Vera*. But Alexander the Great surely demonstrated the highest commitment to the plant. Born in 356 BC in Pella, the ancient capital of Macedonia, Alexander was educated by the philosopher Aristotle.

The most successful ruler in history, Alexander sent *Aloe Vera* direct to the battlefields, where wounded soldiers were treated with its cooling, healing leaves. Alexander was even encouraged by Aristotle to invade and capture the archipelago of Socotra, a trading base in the Indian Ocean. The reason was apparently far from strategic but quite simply to harvest the finest *Aloe Vera* plants.

Morris Men and the Walnut Tree

Dancing in colourful and elaborate costume around a tree wielding sticks and beating the bark might not seem like rational behaviour; it is, however, part of the English Morris Dancing tradition.

Folk dancers, known as Morris Men, have long performed their rituals throughout Britain. The tradition variously involves bells, bows, ribbons, swords, sticks and blackening the face. The origins aren't clear but it is thought to date from the fifteenth century and to be derived from court dancing. At times celebrated as part of the rich rural tapestry, performances were banned under the Puritans because of the links between pagan festivals and the copious consumption of ale. Within the tradition a splinter group, known as Bedlam Morris, were armed with staffs and sticks and performed robust contact dances with each other and, curiously, with trees.

Some of their activities included the rhyme, "The dog, the woman, the walnut tree the more you beat them the better they be!"

While following such advice may be scorned today there are some elements of truth in it. Far from being a spurious and pointless activity, a tree whose bark is damaged in Spring invests considerable resources in repairing the damage, a process that involves the release of growth hormones. It is, in fact, a simple defence mechanism employed by the plant at times of stress. Given the predisposition of all plants to monopolise the niche within which they grow it is perhaps of little surprise that inflicting structural damage to the trunk of a tree provokes a reaction.

In this case the principal hormones released trigger flowering, fruiting and seed production with the aim of safeguarding the population if the parent tree dies. The Morris Dancers simply encourage the tree to produce higher yields of, in this case Walnuts, a valuable, sought-after crop. Gardeners take note that similar threatening behaviour may reap similar rewards on all woody plants, although the wearing of bells and dancing are optional.

Fungus and the French Revolution

It seems implausible that a simple fungus might trigger a revolution in one of the world's most powerful nations but evidence suggests otherwise.

Relentless wars, state bankruptcy, the isolation of the Royal Court, public resentment of absolute rule and frustration at the power of the Church all came to a festering peak in France during the mid 1700s. But it is possible that a little spoken of catalyst could have led to the Peasants' Revolt that sparked the Revolution. Hunger and malnutrition were rife, basic food prices had spiralled and the late 1780s saw several years of devastatingly low harvests caused by the extreme cold and wet weather. In these challenging environmental conditions an unknown and undetected fungal disease swept through the nation. *Claviceps purpurea*, otherwise known as Ergots is a disease of grasses, both wild and cultivated, including Rye, Barley, Oats and Wheat.

Infection occurs via spores that drift on the wind or are splashed by water droplets; cool moist conditions proliferate the attacks. In the host plant the ovary or seed is corrupted and a small purple or black spur-shaped body develops, approximately the size of the original grain.

The developing fungus remains unseen until harvest when grains are milled and are used in staple foods for humans and animals. The consumption of infected grains has startling results. Wild mental aberrations, hallucinations, convulsions, burning skin and joints, miscarriage and sterility were all common. Many people suffered gangrene and limb loss following blood vessel deformation; tremors, manic behaviour, paranoia, loss of speech and death accompanied outbreaks of the disease. It was commonly referred to as St Anthony's Fire or Holy Fire, a reference to the burning sensation experienced during the early stages of infection.

It is named after Saint Anthony who became the accepted father of Christian monasticism thanks in part to his firsthand encounters with the devil. A hermit in Egypt he was responsible for the early organisation of Christian monastic living and famed for his direct combat with the devil and austere journeys into the desert. Contemporaries tell of one encounter with the devil manifesting itself in wild visions, convulsions and near death experiences. Each attack was apparently repelled by Anthony's prayers and penitential acts. Such are the similarities between the symptoms recorded during Anthony's battles with the devil and those induced by ergots that the suggestion is that they were the result of consuming infected wild grains.

Science identifies the active ingredients of ergots as potent alkaloids, the number present depending on the disease strain, host and environmental conditions. Such was the devastation caused by the disease during numerous recorded outbreaks in the late eighteenth century that an estimated 40% of infected people died while up to 75% may have experienced the symptoms. Little wonder then that the French aristocracy were in receipt of the blows and venom of a tormented, terrified peasant population that, in conjunction with other pressures, brought the monarchy to its knees.

Genocide [67]and the Nutmeg

Nutmeg was popularised by the Arabian nations, trading it as an exotic spice through Constantinople from the sixth century. The popularity of this opulently fragrant seed grew as tales of its aphrodisiac properties swept through Europe; patients were advised to rub it liberally onto the genitals to excite sexual passion. And if that were not sufficient to promote the trade of this woody spice of the evergreen Indonesian native tree *Myristica fragrans* it was also said to possess mercurial curative properties. From backache to boils, nausea and even the plague, little resisted the power of nutmeg when carried in a pouch or pocket or pomander.

Such a convincing sales pitch fuelled a frenzied search for the plant amongst wealthy Europeans. King James I of England ordered a voyage to claim the plant, without knowing its origins or geographic whereabouts.

While the search continued the European spice trade became more and more brutal as nations struggled for control of this lucrative market. The Dutch fought the Portuguese for control of the island of Run, one of the Banda Islands in the Indonesian archipelago, the main source of nutmeg and mace, massacring, enslaving and eventually exterminating its entire population.

With a near monopoly prices soared, kept artificially high by the Dutch merchants apparently voluntarily torching supplies to avoid markets being flooded. Displaying a nutmeg became the ultimate symbol of wealth. It was added to food as seasoning leading some members of the nobility to carry personalised miniature graters crafted from precious metals.

Eventually the trade was opened up when the French introduced the plant to Mauritius and the British planted it extensively in Singapore, India, Sri Lanka, the West Indies, and Grenada. Often unrecorded are the underground uses of the nutmeg, viewed by many as poor-man's marijuana. A struggling Charlie Parker, ultimately known as the legendary 'Bird', is said to have introduced its narcotic effects to his band apparently advocating its ingestion as a powder with milk or cola.

That the actions of a woman grieving for a dead child might stimulate an architectural order that that has lasted over 2500 years seems remarkable but according to Vitruvius that is exactly what happened when a woven basket was placed on a grave. It contained modest gifts that had given the young girl pleasure during her short life, and to protect them the grieving mother placed a large tile on top of the basket.

When the architect Callimachus saw the grave the following spring it had been colonised by Acanthus plants and the resulting assemblage was the inspiration for the Corinthian capital. The union of foliage and stone manifested itself in the decoration of Corinthian columns at the Temple of Apollo in Arcadia, ca. 450–420 BC. Apollo the all-powerful god was known as the destroyer and the healer; the plant and its Corinthian decoration quickly became symbolic of the cycle of death, rebirth and immortality.

Adopted and extended to a new order, the Composite, by the Romans, used extensively in Byzantine architecture and the Renaissance, it was revived when Vitruvius was translated in Paris in the seventeenth century. Today, Acanthus leaves are still to be found on palaces, public buildings and stately piles offering a subtext of enduring, stable and immortal existence.

Lettuce may not appear the most exciting food but it has a long history of being linked to lovers. First described in Egyptian tombs, close to where the lettuce grows wild, the plant was considered a sacred aphrodisiac. Greek physicians, however, focussed on the sleep-inducing properties of the wild plant, serving it as a soup at the end of a banquet to enhance the dreams of their guests. Roman Emperor Domitian preferred to test his guests by forcing copious quantities of lettuce upon them to test their rigour and attention. Fall asleep and you might just go the way of the numerous senators and socialites he had executed.

The active ingredient is found in the milky sap that exudes from fractured leaves and stems. More concentrated in the wild forms of lettuce, called Lactuca the milky sap contains high quantities of Lactucarium, a non-narcotic sedative that, like opium, calms the nervous system and induces a euphoric mood. Such properties have not gone unnoticed: in Beatrix Potter's tales Flopsy Bunnies fall asleep after eating Mr McGregor's lettuce.

However, more strangely it is said that some in the Catholic Church suggested the consumption of lettuce sap as a form of contraception. Harvested and dried it was smoked or drunk dissolved in cows' milk to induce a docile state. The results varied in that it allowed some to abandon all inhibitions while in others, especially when consumed in large quantities, it induced deep sleep. While it has no direct contraceptive properties perhaps the ecclesiastical theory was that lovers would fall asleep before passion reached a peak.

Meadows that give Honey Bees Headaches

Medicago sativa may lack familiarity for most but this lowly meadow species provokes great discussion amongst those who have encountered it.

Commonly known as Alfalfa and consumed as sprouted seeds in salads it also goes by the name of Lucerne. Related to the Pea it shares characteristics of basic flower shape, deep roots and leaf shape with many of its relatives. Cultivated since at least 1300 BC in the Middle East it quickly gained favour as a fodder crop, a virtue that is still extolled today by organic farmers around the world. Introduced to Europe via trade it spread into South America as a reliable animal feed for the Conquistadors.

Roman attention was rapidly aroused and writings celebrating the plant as early as 4AD noted the viability of the crop and its ability to make impoverished soils 'sweet'. Called Medica after the Medes, a tribe from Persia where the plant originated, the modern scientific name is a reference to those early notes. Early observations might be innocent but the sweetening of the soils can be explained by the plant's ability to harvest nitrogen from the atmosphere, storing it as nodules on its roots. In turn this harvested nitrogen, one of the three major nutrients for plant growth, is made available to other plants, so enriching the ground. It is this principle of soil self-enrichment that forms the basis of modern organic farming practices.

However, the crop comes with some headaches – literally – as it seems that the shape of the flower, with a generous landing platform and large upper petal, known as the keel, poses something of a challenge for the European Honey Bee. Enticed to the plant in search of nectar rewards the bee is neither sufficiently heavy to prise the bloom open, nor small enough to crawl in. Consequently, as it attempts to scrabble towards the nectaries at the rear of the flower, the bee is repeatedly bludgeoned by the heavy keel, which causes some distress and means that pollination rarely occurs. It seems that juvenile bees learning the trade persevere with the head banging while older, more experienced members of the hive simply bypass the petals and get their nectar meal by chewing a hole through the rear of the flower. This apparent oversight in evolution is attributed to the fact that the Alfalfa has evolved with a specific relationship to a different bee.

Not content with frustrating a population of bees the Alfalfa is also under the spotlight when it comes to animal fertility. Known to be high in phytoestrogens, compounds that are known to cause estrogenic effects in animals, researchers are following leads that indicate a reduction of fertility in sheep, quail and parrots that feed on a diet of Alfalfa.

71
Mistletoe Kisses and the Gods

An innocent kiss under the Mistletoe (*Viscum album*) is widespread in the West as an integral part of the Christmas festivities. It has long played a part in ritual and courtship but perhaps not as innocently as we assume. For the Ancient Druids mistletoe was a sacred plant. The Chief Druid would cut the mistletoe from the Oak using a golden sickle on the sixth night of the new moon after the winter solstice. Cloths were held beneath the tree to ensure that the plant did not touch the ground. The cut branches were then divided into sprigs for villagers to hang over doorways as protection against thunder, lightning and other assorted evils. Miraculous results were expected of the plant: it was thought to cure all illnesses, and to guarantee good health.

Throughout the centuries the tradition morphed into numerous guises: enemies laid down arms under mistletoe; Anglo Saxons kissed under is boughs as a sign of friendship; while in France a kiss under it on New Year's Day indicated future marriage.

But there was more to the collection and displaying of mistletoe. As the Druids observed, the plant produces milky white berries only on the female plant, the male producing nothing more than yellow blooms in spring. Berry-carrying plants were sacred to pre-Christian Europeans and the sap from these viscous fruits was heralded as from the very loins of the woodland gods and was consequently regarded as semen to be revered. Applied to a suitor it was the purest form of aphrodisiac and a kiss under the influence of the plant ensured a favourable outcome.

Not for all the Tea in China

The dour Scot Robert Fortune was despatched on one of the greatest espionage missions of history to defraud a nation and enhance the power of a British colony. His mission was to steal the secret of tea production. His horticultural skills were honed at the Royal Botanic Garden, Edinburgh and from 1842 as Superintendent of the Hothouse Department at the Horticultural Society's garden at Chiswick, London. His meteoric rise continued when in 1843, after a four-month voyage he found himself in Hong Kong as the Society's Head Collector in China with a daunting list of target plants to collect in a country where hostility towards the British was extreme in the aftermath of the first Opium War.

His mission to bring new plants (*Camellia Sinensis*) was successful and he was sent on a second mission in 1842. Major Chinese trading ports were now open and England had acquired Hong Kong. Clearly ingenuity was called for as Fortune's aim was to travel to the most private gardens of the Emperor and steal prized plants including the finest peaches. Pirates, disease, tropical storms and muggers were no match for him; he eventually returned to England in 1845 with many exotic flowers never before seen in England.

While his first trip centred on horticultural curiosities, the plan for his second trip, in 1848, reads like the plot of a spy thriller; he was to infiltrate, undetected, the most sacred and secretive sites in the heartlands of a hostile China and steal centuries-old secrets on the cultivation and production of tea, one of the world's most sought after commodities on which the great wealth of China was based. He was then to cross the border into India, preferably with live tea plants. His daring exploits were to be funded by the hugely powerful East India Company, which then controlled trade in India.

He succeeded in purchasing or stealing young tea plants, on occasion hiding them within the folds of his long robes. After amassing the technical knowhow necessary for tea production and some 20,000 young plants, Fortune walked into India in 1851 bringing tea to Darjeeling and ending China's total dominance of the tea trade.

What is often untold is the direct consequence of the crippling of China's export trade and increased hostility to the 'foreign devils' that resulted in the second Opium War in which France, Russia and the United States all became embroiled and which eventually, in 1860, forced the total capitulation and humiliation of China.

Pineapple and Cannibals

Accepted in Europe as the ultimate symbol of hospitality, early encounters with the Pineapple were far from pleasurable. A member of the Bromeliad family originating from the border regions of Brazil and Paraguay it is uncertain quite how the domesticated form of this rosette-forming herbaceous perennial found its way to the Caribbean islands where Europeans first encountered it.

What is in little doubt is the point at which Europeans observed the plant. On 24th September 1493 when Christopher Columbus set off from the Canary Islands on his second voyage to the Caribbean the principal aim was not necessarily only to pillage the discovered lands but to assess their potential for colonisation. When berthing off the coast of Guadeloupe in the first week of November of the same year his troops observed large vats in which human remains were evident. While pursuing the native, much feared Caribs through the local flora, tethered sacrificial humans were commonly reported, clearly indicating cannibalistic activity. Wherever human sacrifice was taking place the exotic fruit of the Pineapple was also evident, as slices, peelings or stockpiled. Quite what role the plant played was unclear to the marauding army. Perplexed and curious about this succulent, sweet and unique fruit that the locals referred to as 'Anana' meaning 'excellent fruit', Columbus's men sent samples of it home as booty, officially introducing the Pineapple to European kitchens in the autumn of 1494.

Perhaps what was missed in those early encounters was the process in which the Pineapple was employed. The Carib tribes sliced and diced fresh fruits to form the base of a marinade sauce that was applied to the hapless human sacrifice. After due seasoning and a little light heat a celebratory banquet was served to assembled dignitaries. Such gory detail may have been omitted in the retelling of discovery stories at the courts of Renaissance Europe but what persisted was a fascination with the fruit: it was held as a prized possession with motifs finding

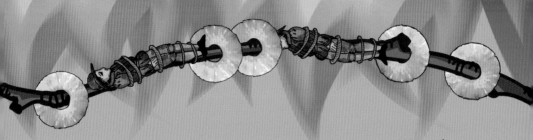

their way onto tapestry, art, carvings, stone finials and of course as a centrepiece at banquets. A trade even existed in hiring out the fruits while gardeners toiled to perfect cultivation. Eventually, two hundred years after its introduction into Europe the first Pineapple was successfully harvested and its elevation from cannibal seasoning to Royal patronage was complete when in 1675 Hendrik Danckerts painted Charles II of England being presented with the first pineapple grown in England by his royal gardener, John Rose, as a token of loyalty and friendship.

Curiously, while the nobility clamoured for the fruits, the act of serving pineapple as a meat garnish has prevailed: no traditional English pub would be respected if Gammon, Pineapple and Chips were absent from the menu. Quite why this tradition started is lost in the kitchens of time but the Carib tribes had deduced quite correctly that

a sinewy individual would be made more palatable by the fruits, a process initiated by the enzyme bromelian, this being of sufficient concentration in ripe fruits to break down fats and tenderise flesh. So next time you are tempted to order Gammon and Pineapple spare a thought for the unfortunate victims in ancient Guadeloupe who in no small way assisted in the creation of this pub grub.

Pond Weed Power

Imagine a scenario in which green scum that resembles primordial soup offers the secret of sustainable power for technologically advanced flight, sophisticated personnel rockets and sprawling 25th century cities. Is this science fiction or a glimpse of the future?

Born in 1902, Hans Gaffron, a photosynthetic research scientist who graduated from Berlin University in 1925 created a scientific model of an idealised world in which all energy was derived from the simplest form of life, single-celled algae. Gaffron fled Nazi Germany in 1937 and worked extensively at the University of Chicago and as professor of biochemistry and plant physiology at the Institute of Molecular Biophysics in Tallahassee, Florida.

For thirty years he studied the way in which *Chlamydomonas reinhardtii*, a ubiquitous single-celled algae could be encouraged, in controlled conditions, to switch from the production of oxygen during photosynthesis, as demonstrated by all green plants, to the production of hydrogen. This potential revolution would allow not only the harvesting of hydrogen fuel but also the sustainable generation of electricity with little or no pollutants. The problem was the very short periods during which the algae could be persuaded to create hydrogen.

The breakthrough occurred in 1999 when a University of California, Berkeley professor called Tasios Melis revealed that the deprivation of oxygen and sulphur was the key to switching on hydrogen production in algae. Simply altering the growing environment temporarily provoked the required reaction, and by carefully controlling the sulphur supply to the algae, which uses sulphur in the production of proteins, they were able to deliver hydrogen and survive indefinitely.

A 500-litre algae bioreactor was subsequently constructed and, under the necessary modified conditions, the algae produced one litre of hydrogen per hour with just water and sunlight. Melis estimates that the bioreactor was running at about 10% efficiency and anticipates elevating it to 50% or more. Achieve this and 25th century sustainable clean energy could be a 21st century reality.

Popeye's Poor Maths Report

The iconic image of Popeye first appeared in 1929 in the United States in a comic called *Thimble Theatre*. By the early 1930s he was firmly established as an All-American favourite, gorging on Spinach to fuel his powers. A peculiar fascination with this Asian leaf crop was stimulated by American research dating back to the early 1900s, which singled out Spinach as being a hundred times more potent in nutritionally beneficial iron than any other plant tested. This was just the ammunition the US government needed and it sparked a drive for healthy eating based on this miracle crop.

The nation's obsession with the leaf grew rapidly and in 1937 the Spinach growers of Crystal City, Texas erected a statue in celebration of the comic hero after their industry experienced an unprecedented 30% increase in trade. By 1941 Popeye had been enlisted in the war effort, joining the Navy, and appearing in an all-white uniform. The appeal of the Spinach-munching hero continues today; he even has his own theme park and branded Bloomingdales products.

However, explore the 1900s' dietary analysis and the reputation of the pipe-smoking, tattooed muscle man looks a little problematic. No spike of iron was present in the initial findings causing some to question the legitimacy of the later report and the independence of its sponsors. Clearly, foul play is a possibility but in fact the simple explanation lies in the arithmetic ineptitude of a junior clerk who managed to put a decimal point in the wrong place while collating the results. As a consequence of this debacle Spinach gained an unjust reputation and Popeye's heroics wowed the world.

Curiously, Spinach does contain good levels of iron but it also contains oxalates, a compound of oxalic acid and iron or calcium. In this form the iron is ejected in the urine, leaving the oxalates. High oxalate levels have been linked to kidney disorders, gout and rheumatoid arthritis so it seems that as Popeye joins the octogenarians he may not be in such fine fettle.

Potpourri-drugged Olympian

Perhaps not the most controversial of interior decorations there is little to suggest anything untoward in a fragrant bowl of dried seeds and leaves unless, that is, you were competing at the 1904 Olympics.

Derived from a seventeenth-century French concept of collecting living plant material, allowing it to wilt and then dousing it in salt to preserve it, potpourri was often a mouldy collection of exotic blooms, fruits and seeds from the expanding Empire, an expression of sophistication and status. Fragrance was added in autumn in the form of spices and herbs before the concoction was placed in rooms to add pleasant aromas.

Potpourri, or at least one of its contents sparked controversy during the marathon of the St Louis Olympics when in searing heat and humidity the field of 32 headed out into the countryside. Hindered by horse carts, ruts and a lack of facilities except a water tower and a roadside well, most abandoned the race and several fell unconscious at the roadside. The race was won by the American Fred Lorz, but as President Roosevelt's daughter Alice was about to present the gold medal officials were informed that Lorz had driven most of the way in a car, only running the final five miles.

Next to cross the finishing line was British-born athlete Thomas Hicks competing for the United States. He crossed the line but then collapsed. Awarded the gold medal he was carried from the stadium a hero until it was discovered that his trainer, Charles Lucas had administered several grains of strychnine concealed in egg whites to his charge during the race.

Derived from the plant *Strychnos nux-nomica*, a native of India and south-east Asia, the fruits and seeds are rich in alkaloid toxins including strychnine. Once the orange fruits are opened, platelike seeds with a distinctive sheen are revealed. It is these that have been widely included in many potpourri collections for their decorative appeal. Suggestions abound that Lucas obtained his strychnine from the seeds found in potpourri and although he never admitted its source it is known that he experimented and boasted about his development of various performance enhancing drugs.

Lucas should clearly have concentrated on interior decoration since the application of strychnine is highly dangerous, causing convulsions, nausea, corruption of the central nervous system and spasms. No wonder reporters recorded that Hicks looked ashen on crossing the line.

Rocketing "Mother-in-Law" into Space

NASA research shows that the principal challenge in creating a sustainable space station is the long term supply of clean air and the solution lies in your 'Mother-in-Law's Tongue'. This ubiquitous succulent houseplant, correctly known as Sansevieria originates in Africa, India and Indonesia. After years of research and billon-dollar technology programmes, the solution was found naturalised outside the NASA research offices.

Sansevieria has proved the most effective and efficient agent, natural or artificial, for scrubbing away over 107 pollutants. It neutralises highly toxic pollutants including benzene, a known mutagen and carcinogen found in petrol, paints, inks and rubber; Trichloroethylene used in printing inks, paints, lacquers, varnishes and adhesives and considered carcinogenic; and Formaldehyde, which is thought to cause asthma and is present in particle board, waxed papers, facial tissues and paper towels, household cleaning agents, floor coverings, carpet backings and cigarette smoke.

How such toxins are absorbed into the tissues of the plant is easily understood since all plants rely on gaseous exchange to facilitate photosynthesis. This is primarily achieved by opening pores, known as stomata, on the leaf tissue and as a consequence oxygen, water vapour and carbon dioxide are all exchanged, alongside the toxins preoccupying NASA. Once inside the plant, toxins are converted into harmless compounds and deposited via the roots into the soil, a process involving not only the plant but also calling on the services of soil bacteria. So effective is Sansevieria that it has been suggested that one mature plant with a minimum of five leaves can cleanse a room of 100 cubic metres.

Not surprisingly, it is now being considered as a cleansing agent for offices with 'Sick Building Syndrome', so it might be a good idea to take your Mother-in-Law's Tongue to work with you.

The Roman Nettle March

Roman soldiers are well documented as being capable of marching in formation for many miles with some estimates suggesting that 20-30 miles a day were expected. However, progress slowed when they encountered the inclement weather of northern Europe, considerably cooler and damper than the southern Mediterranean climate many were used to, although modern research into stalactite development, isotopes in molluscs, pollen grains and glacial demise indicates that the average temperature for the period from 1-400 AD was up to 5° warmer than today.

Cold limbs, the onset of rheumatism and arthritis provoked misery amongst the troops. Recently unearthed tablets at Vindolanda near Hadrian's Wall contain requests for extra provisions – the most popular being socks or soccus as they were then called, loose-fitting slippers worn under sandals.

The Roman soldiers also recruited the services of the Roman Nettle (*Urtica pilulifera*), a more robust, stately and energetic form than the British native Nettle and named after the latin 'uro' meaning to burn or, rather more tellingly, to irritate by burning. Its medicinal, culinary, dying and fibre-producing properties were described by Pliny, all providing justification for transporting and harvesting the plant, but an alternative use explains why Nettle seeds were carried and planted by each legion. When mature, the foliage was harvested, mounted on staffs and used to whip the legs and feet of the soldiers.

As any child knows mature Nettle foliage causes a burning rash, as a result of the formic acid released when hairs on the leaf come into contact with skin. One side effect of the nettle sting is the stimulation of blood flow to the affected area, causing a feeling of warmth. By whipping their soldiers not only did the Romans alleviate their cold feet but also inadvertently highlighted modern scientific advantages of this ubiquitous weed.

Formic acid is used in homeopathic medicines to ease conditions such as arthritis; recent research has demonstrated that Nettle leaves used daily on the hands of arthritis sufferers for a week produced both an immediate and prolonged reduction in arthritic pain. Current research into the Nettle is attempting to determine what role the formic acid plays and if the histamine and serotonin of the Nettle act as neuro-transmitters.

121

Roses cross Napoleonic Blockades

Empress Joséphine of France, the first wife of Napoleon Bonaparte was a passionate gardener with huge aspirations. In 1797, while he was absent on the Egyptian campaign she bought an old, rundown 150-acre estate just 12 kilometres from Paris called the Château de Malmaison. On his return she convinced Napoleon to invest heavily in the renovation of the estate including the remodelling of the extensive grounds.

Joséphine was passionate about natural history and well connected with botanists and collectors of the day so the parkland soon became filled with exotica of the period. Zebra, Antelope, Ostrich and Kangaroo all graced the grounds while orangeries, tropical glasshouses and pineapple houses provided flowers and culinary delights. Many plants introduced into cultivation at the time were first planted at Malmaison including species from Asia and South America. Magnolia, Paeonia, Camellia, Dahlia and Hibiscus all prospered in the pampered environment. The finest explorers were patronised by Joséphine in pursuit of her expanding collection including Nicolas Baudin, famed for his trips to Chile, Peru, the Pacific Islands and Australia from where he introduced 2500 species to Western science.

Perhaps most horticulturally pioneering was Joséphine's creation of a Rose garden at the heart of her fashionable *jardin à l'anglaise*. Prior to her passion for the Rose it was largely confined to modest alcoves; her approach centred the Rose in the garden and the Rose garden in the landscape. She was instrumental in the reawakening of the modern gardener's love of the Rose. This was a time when the old, familiar species of *Rosa gallica*, Damask and Alba, all close derivatives of wild roses were joined by flamboyant, exotic species from China. Breeding of these new roses led directly to an explosion of garden-worthy plants thanks to the China Rose's perpetual flowering, vibrant foliage and varied colours. Portland, Bourbon and China Tea roses, so

called because of their fragrance with a hint of tea, are all descendants of plants Joséphine would have been familiar with in her collection.

Within ten years she had amassed some 250 varieties, 120 of them captured in the paintings of her protégé and official artist Pierre-Joseph Redouté.

Unfortunately for Joséphine, the majority of the finest cultivars were being raised in English nurseries and England and France were at war. But Joséphine was notoriously determined and did not let the war or the total blockades on trade and shipping deter her. Records show that any French ships captured by the English were allowed to continue on their voyage if they were carrying consignments of Roses for the gardens at Malmaison, remarkable given the ingrained hostility between the two nations. Perhaps as surprising are accounts of the *jardin à l'anglaise* name being retained throughout the period despite all reference to English culture being despised in France.

Joséphine's passion for the Rose should come as no surprise since she was born Marie-Josèphe-Rose Tascher and was always called Rose during her early life. She was forced to adopt the name Joséphine when she met the young Napoleon, who disliked the name Rose.

A Panacea or Life or at least Grey Hair

Any plant that is claimed to derive from the gardens of creatures that are half man half goat, that revel in sex, drink and boisterous parties is sure to provoke a frown. The Common Sage (*Salvia officinalis*) is just such a plant, ubiquitous in herb gardens and most frequently encountered in the stuffing inside roast poultry. In this guise it is the accompaniment most diners reluctantly graze on before concealing what is left under sprouts and gravy so as not to cause offence to the chef.

But there is a wealth of stifled talent wrapped within the leaves of Sage. For classicists, the Latin name says it all: it is derived from 'salvere', to be saved. The Romans, Greeks and Arabs all claimed that it offered immortality; perhaps overselling its potential a little, but history abounds with more modest claims. "Why should a man die while he grows sage in his garden?" we read in European Medieval texts. Sage as saviour, life preserver, and panacea are all common concepts. Herbalists, perhaps not the most

objective of critics, throughout the globe are universally supportive citing it as a cure for head, brain, sight, sickness and stomach ailments.

The Chinese, who pioneered herbal medicine and for whom the Sage was not a native plant, attempted to trade it, at times offering three times the weight of their most choice tea in exchange.

Modern research does not contest many of these outlandish claims. The oil extracted from Sage contains plentiful hydrocarbons, including Salvene, and offers antibacterial, antiseptic, stimulant, mood enhancing and stress busting properties. The list of ailments in which the plant offers relief reads like an A-Z, including sore throat, ulcers, bleeding gums, cooling of fevers, skin cleanser, blood purifier, delirium relief, stomach tonic, typhoid relief, liver cleanser, measles, palsy and joint pain.

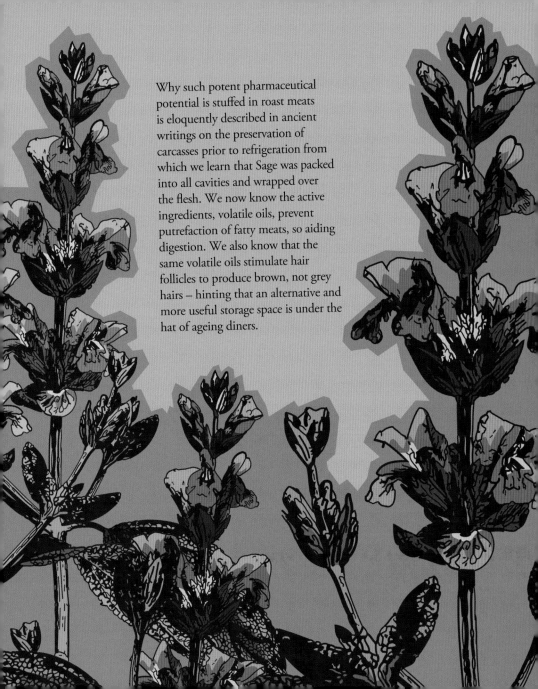

Why such potent pharmaceutical potential is stuffed in roast meats is eloquently described in ancient writings on the preservation of carcasses prior to refrigeration from which we learn that Sage was packed into all cavities and wrapped over the flesh. We now know the active ingredients, volatile oils, prevent putrefaction of fatty meats, so aiding digestion. We also know that the same volatile oils stimulate hair follicles to produce brown, not grey hairs – hinting that an alternative and more useful storage space is under the hat of ageing diners.

⁸¹Salvation of the Olive

The Olive tree (*Olea europea*) is synonymous with healthy Mediterranean diets and has long been cultivated in the region with petrified groves dating back 60,000 years. Considered a sacred tree, it was highly protected. Aristotle stated that the penalty for killing an Olive tree was death; he also retained a secret Olive grove whose oil was provided only to Olympic athletes.

Symbolizing good health and longevity, the Olive was woven into the first Olympic crowns, and to symbolise the unity of competitors the first Olympic torches were made of Olive wood. In Greek mythology the Olive tree was considered a beacon of peace and prosperity, blessed by Athena, the ancient goddess of wisdom. No surprise then that Noah learned of peace returning to earth when a dove returned with an Olive branch.

Raw oil was used as lamp oil to keep the sacred flames in temples burning. The fact that Olive oil naturally resists oxidation made it the ideal medium to preserve foods and medicines, a tradition that persists unrivalled today. Olive oil also played a key role in medicine, not only thanks to its own properties, but also as a basis for innumerable healing oils and salves. Considered a supernatural substance, which served as a sacred consecration oil to purify the body in honour of the gods, the effect of massaging the salve or oil on the skin and hair to make it glisten was regarded as an attribute of beauty. Unoiled skin and dry hair were considered unsavoury and unhealthy so athletes were always thoroughly coated prior to the Games. The term 'salve' morphed into an ancient Greek greeting, translated as 'may you be oiled', which has given us the word salvation.

Say it with Flowers

When Europe's explorers went looking for the riches of the East, they found the West. They also stumbled upon a treasure in Peru and Bolivia that would ultimately prove to be more valuable than gold or spice, the Potato (*Solanum tuberosum*). Introduced into Britain and Spain around the middle of the sixteenth century, Potatoes were not grown widely until the end of the seventeenth. Frederick William I of Prussia planted them in his garden in Berlin, and clearly they had an impact as his son Frederick II continued the practice growing them using peasant labour.

Prussian tastes for the Potato were out of step with the rest of Europe. The Portuguese, Spanish and French had ideal growing conditions but were suspicious of the unfamiliar tuber. The French even went as far as banning the plant's cultivation from 1748 because they thought it caused leprosy. Meanwhile agriculturalists considered the plant a garden novelty and struggled to work out how it could be incorporated into the plough, sow, harvest, graze cycle that was common farming practice throughout Europe.

Support principally emanated from an unlikely source: Antoine-Augustin Parmentier, appointed by Napoleon in 1805 as the Inspector General of the Health Service. Parmentier pioneered the chemistry of nutrition, explored the extraction of sugar from beets, investigated how to store foods and was instrumental in popularising vaccines for smallpox. His encounter with the Potato followed his capture by the Prussians during the Seven Year War, a conflict embroiling all the major powers of the world in a dispute between, on one side the French and Spanish, and on the other the British and the House of Hanover. During his imprisonment Parmentier was fed on Potatoes, then used only as pig feed by the French.

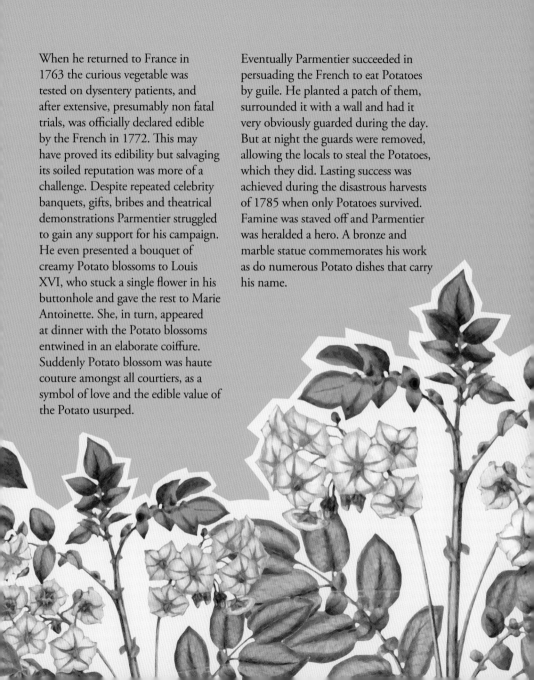

When he returned to France in 1763 the curious vegetable was tested on dysentery patients, and after extensive, presumably non fatal trials, was officially declared edible by the French in 1772. This may have proved its edibility but salvaging its soiled reputation was more of a challenge. Despite repeated celebrity banquets, gifts, bribes and theatrical demonstrations Parmentier struggled to gain any support for his campaign. He even presented a bouquet of creamy Potato blossoms to Louis XVI, who stuck a single flower in his buttonhole and gave the rest to Marie Antoinette. She, in turn, appeared at dinner with the Potato blossoms entwined in an elaborate coiffure. Suddenly Potato blossom was haute couture amongst all courtiers, as a symbol of love and the edible value of the Potato usurped.

Eventually Parmentier succeeded in persuading the French to eat Potatoes by guile. He planted a patch of them, surrounded it with a wall and had it very obviously guarded during the day. But at night the guards were removed, allowing the locals to steal the Potatoes, which they did. Lasting success was achieved during the disastrous harvests of 1785 when only Potatoes survived. Famine was staved off and Parmentier was heralded a hero. A bronze and marble statue commemorates his work as do numerous Potato dishes that carry his name.

The Queen's Water Lily Palace

Never shying away from adventure in the name of the Crown, nor from exaggerating the sights and experiences on those adventures, the Victorian explorers were a curious bunch. Many told tales of man-eating plants, skyscraping trees and devilish creatures, partly as proof of their courage but also to attract potential patrons. One of the few who had little need to embellish his adventures was Sir Robert Schomburgk.

German born but exploring the globe on behalf of the British he ventured into the perilous Amazon basin in 1837 discovering a monster water lily in Guiana. Claiming it as a first he introduced it to Europe; curiously history has conveniently forgotten that it had previously been recorded and described by his fellow German Eduard Friedrich Poeppig.

A race ensued to cultivate this remarkable plant, and to present Queen Victoria with the first flowers. Originally known as *Victoria regia*, literally 'Queen Victoria', the plant, now called *Victoria amazonica*, requires not only rich fertile waters, but also bright light, tropical temperatures and pools of oceanic proportions to accommodate its 8m long stems and 3m diameter leaves that, in the same way as its water lily relatives, sit in the water like an archipelago. First prize for presenting a royal flower went to the Duke of Devonshire who having shown little aptitude for gardening suddenly employed the services of Kew-educated Joseph Paxton as head gardener and architect Decimus Burton to build a glass edifice to house the gargantuan plant. The resulting conservatory was 87m long, 37m wide and 19m high and was described as a 'sea of glass', and a 'tropical scene with a glass sky'. It cost over £33,000. The reward, however, was the first flower of *Victoria regia*.

Such was the size of the plant that Paxton became curious about the leaf construction. The upper surface is tissue paper like in texture but it is supported underneath by a labyrinth of ever-thickening structural veins and savage spines. Paxton was so impressed with the plant's structure that he famously stood his daughter Alice in the middle of a free floating lily pad. Sketching out the precise architecture of the leaf Paxton submitted to Prince Albert a revolutionary design for a glasshouse and was awarded the contract to build the greatest ever glasshouse, the Crystal Palace. Opened in 1851 for the Great Exhibition the entire building was inspired by the leaf of the monster lily from the Amazon.

The Spirit of Christmas – upside down

The Spruce (*Picea abies*) is popularly considered the original Christmas tree but the tradition of felling a conifer and hauling it indoors to be festooned with garlands and gifts strangely has nothing to do with the celebration of Christmas. Informal decoration of trees, especially evergreen species, in the wooded landscapes of northern Europe was practised by ancient tribes who observed that some trees retained their foliage despite the severity of winter and proclaimed these mysterious specimens the home of mischievous woodland sprites. To appease the sprites and ensure good fortune during the shortest days of the year, gifts were ceremoniously hung on the branches of the evergreens, rendering the plants sacred. The tradition of never felling a Holly persists to this day. The Romans honoured Saturn, the god of agriculture by hanging polished metals in trees during the winter festival of Saturnalia and throughout the Middle Ages in Europe the Feast of Adam and Eve on 24th December was celebrated by hanging wild apples on a fir tree to create a 'Paradise Tree'. But in the eighth century the custom was almost turned upside down by St. Boniface, who travelled from Wessex (now Devon) in England to Thuringia in Germany as a missionary. He adopted the symbol of an upside down fir tree as a simple triangular form, to explain the principle of the Holy Trinity to the pagan tribes whose decorations celebrated woodland fairies. So the concept of felling tree tops and hanging them upside down had permeated much of mainland Europe by the twelfth century, persisting in Germany and Austria until the eighteenth century.

Why or when the Christmas tree was set right side up again is not known but by the early nineteenth century the practice of exhibiting and decorating a Christmas tree was common among the Prussian nobility. Viewed as a Protestant custom it was widely rejected by the Catholic faith and even viewed with suspicion by Protestant churches, which disapproved of trees in churches until the 1900s. When Queen Charlotte of the House of Hanover married King George III of England she brought the Christmas tree with her but it did not become popular in the country until Queen Victoria married Prince Albert, who shared with her the delight of his own Christmas experience.

Vanilla – the Elixir for Impotence

Few would suspect that the World's most popular ice cream flavour was also a potent aphrodisiac. However, the results of a German survey in 1762 revealed that all the 342 patients treated with Vanilla extract were instantly, and presumably pleasantly, cured. What the medication was, or indeed how it was applied, has been lost in time. This is not the only account of vanilla's powers to titillate and arouse. Ancient Aztec stories tell of Xanat, the young daughter of the Mexican fertility goddess, who loved a lowly Totonac boy. Unable to marry him because of her divine nature, she transformed herself into a plant that would provide him with pleasure and happiness.

The Totonac people of Mexico were producers of the finest Vanilla's until the nineteenth century. The plant had been introduced into Europe by the Spanish Conquistadors but cultivation had proved impossible. The Spanish, Dutch and French all stole plants to introduce them into their colonies in the hope of capturing the market. But although the plants thrived no Vanilla could be harvested. The challenge for early horticulturalists was how to ensure the production of seed pods as it is the seeds that encapsulate the exotic flavours, a complex blend of over 400 compounds.

What the colonists had not realised was that the Vanilla plant had evolved in a symbiotic relationship with Humming Birds and Melipone Bees. Only these forest creatures could pollinate the flower. Remove the plant from the forest and pollination is impossible. The problem was finally solved in 1841 by a chance discovery by a twelve-year-old African slave, Edmond Albius, who lived in the French territory of Réunion Island. Using a thin splinter of wood to simulate the action of the Melipone Bee, he prised the complex flower open to allow contact between the anther and the stigma; self-pollination occurred and the flower faded. Each plant produces an abundance of blooms in pendant racemes but only one bloom opens per day on each raceme. Pollination of more than five blooms per raceme destroys quality so growers ensure each plant produces no more than fifty or so pods per year. They take over nine months to ripen. Despite being time consuming and laborious the technique discovered by Edmond Albius is still used today throughout the world. It is surely one of the great ironies that a plant revered for so long as an aphrodisiac must be artificially pollinated. Despite kickstarting a multi-million pound industry Albius remained poverty stricken and died destitute in 1880.

Victory Wreaths and Cyanide

The long held tradition of placing a wreath of Laurel leaves on the head of a victorious competitor goes back to the ancients but where once our heroes were decked in glorious foliage, we now opt for toxic alternatives.

Placing wreaths around the neck or on the head of a competitor originates in the arduous competitions in Grecian stadiums. The wreath was initiated at the ancient Olympic games in honour of Zeus, king of the gods and defender of Olympus from the onslaught of the Gigantes, a tribe of one hundred giants born of Gaia the Earth from the blood of the castrated Ouranos.

Originally the wreath was made of Olive, but the influence of the Pythian games, held in the years between the Olympic games, led to the universal acceptance of the Sweet Bay (*Laurus nobilis*), a highly scented evergreen tree of the region, the essential oils of which stimulate the mind, tune the senses and foster great bravery. Associated with Apollo, healer and god of music, poetry, plague, oracles, sun, medicine, light and knowledge to name but few, a branch of Bay was the only prize a successful competitor could expect, although later an apple supplemented this meagre prize for some. The transition from branch to wreath was introduced by the Romans, for whom the Bay also symbolised Apollo but poetry of the day tells of the god wearing a wreath of Bay as an emblem of unrequited love for the Greek nymph Daphne, whose father turned her into a Bay tree to prevent his advances. Hence the plant's associations with undying affection, love and protection. Traditionally lovers exchanged Bay in bouquets, as Roman soldiers did with their families prior to battle, a tradition continued today in funeral wreaths.

The protection Bay offered permeated Western culture. Seventeenth-century herbalist Culpeper wrote, "Neither witch nor devil, thunder nor lightning, will hurt a man in the place where a Bay tree is." It is still common to plant Bay at the door of the home for protection from evil.

Today's sporting heroes may receive ample reward for their endeavours but the noble origins of the wreath are hidden as modern ones are made from Laurel (*Prunus laurocerasus*), a noxious, toxic and invasive weed. All parts of the plant contain high values of hydrogen cyanide, a poison that is released by bruising or crushing leaves, seeds or blooms and one characterised by a putrid almond scent that can cause respiratory failure and death.

The Violet, the Corporal and his Martinique Lover

The Violet is perhaps dubiously honoured as the morosest of blooms, one enshrined in desperate stories of love lost and lives left destitute. In Ancient Greece the mythological figure Io, the lover of Jupiter was turned into a heifer by the king of the gods to avoid the vitriol of his wife. As she roamed the region the footsteps of the forlorn Io are marked by the emergence of Violets. Perhaps the amiable and tranquil persona of Io led to the adoption of the Violet as the guardian of sleep, peace and serenity. No story better encapsulates the desperate Violet in real life than that of Napoleon and his first wife Joséphine de Beauharnais. The Parma Violet with its delicately sweet fragrance was popular in the posies, worn loose on the breast at the royal courts of the day. It was one of Joséphine's favourite flowers, often embroidered on her dresses.

The upwardly mobile Napoleon met Joséphine in 1795, fell in love and embarked on a deluge of love letters to the woman he eventually married in 1796. But Joséphine was a complex woman. Born on the French colony of Martinique to a bankrupt aristocratic family she lacked the sophistication of courtly ladies. Marked throughout her life by blackened teeth, thought to derive from a childhood diet rich in sugar, she embarked on an arranged marriage to a Parisian Viscount, but after two children was abandoned by her husband who openly stated his repulsion for her. To maintain her connections Joséphine became mistress to the social and political elite, a lucrative, prolonged and varied career that funded her extravagant lifestyle. It was as a mistress that she eventually met Napoleon.

After a wedding dress and ceremony festooned in Violets Joséphine, less than enamoured with Napoleon, reverted to her role as mistress. Napoleon, aware of his wife's misdemeanours, continued his letters, sometimes loving, occasionally desperate, often highly erotic, but eventually realised that the heir he so desperately desired would not be provided by the ageing Joséphine. He ended the marriage in 1809; she filled the Rose garden at Malmaison, her country estate, with Violets. Within a year Napoleon was married to Archduchess Marie Louise of Austria and an heir was born.

But Napoleon's heart remained true to Joséphine. In exile on the Isle of Elba in 1814 he declared to his supporters that he would return when the Violets were back in bloom. Bonapartists chose the Violet as their emblem and nicknamed Napoleon *le Caporal la Violette*. Postcards picturing a bunch of violets soon flooded France, but when close inspection revealed the outline portrait of Napoleon the French government banned any reproduction of the Violet until after 1874.

Joséphine died on 29 May 1814. On hearing of her death Napoleon refused to leave his room for two days. When he eventually returned to France the following February, he went straight to Malmaison and picked Violets from her garden, scattering some on her grave and placing others in a locket that he wore until his death.

Walnut Shells and the RAF

The thought of firing Walnuts into an engine might seem preposterous but it was a practice regularly used during the Second World War by engineers who were well aware that efficiency relied on the machine being finely tuned. Experiments demonstrated that the most effective method of cleansing the internal pistons and cranks was to deploy the woody shells of the Walnut (*Juglans regia*).

The idea quickly caught on and was widely adopted by the automotive industry and manufacturers of fine gearing systems. To facilitate the operation the shell of the Walnut was ground down into progressively smaller particles ranging from sand to flour in texture. Essentially the Walnut retains an angular particle, no matter how finely ground and it is this, along with its consistency that ensures effective cleansing.

According to the Mohs scale of hardness the walnut rates at 3-4, placing it above many minerals but well below quartz and diamond. It also falls below steel, making it a minimal abrasive cleaner, essential to the longevity of the engine. Today Walnuts are fired into the world's most sophisticated gas turbines, jet engines, and gearing systems continuing the process started by ingenious RAF engineers.

You might also come across its abrasive qualities in drilling operations, as a non-slip agent in paints, as a chemical scrubber in flues or chimneys, as a powder carrier in agricultural insecticides, and even as a filler in dynamite.

William of Orange's Root Vegetable Encounter

Ask most gardeners what colour a Carrot (*Daucus carota*) is and the answer will be orange. However, the orange Carrot is a relatively recent addition to our diet. Despite being present in pollen records dating back 55 million years, its precise history is not fully understood. The Eastern carrot, identified by its purple and/or yellow branched root, grey-green leaves and early flowering habit came from Afghanistan and was taken into Spain by Moorish invaders in the twelfth century. Early references to Carrots tend to be confused, but the colour orange is not mentioned until the sixteenth century and not popularised until the seventeenth century. Orange forms possibly arose as a result of mutations of yellow, aided by selection and breeding undertaken in the Netherlands. Research shows that the broad genetic pool of the modern Carrot contains yellow-rooted Eastern carrots, the cultivated white-rooted Carrot from Western medicinal gardens and, finally, wild European species. Quite why there was a drive for an orange form is not documented.

However, the emergence of the orange Carrot occurred in the Netherlands and coincided with the rise of the Protestant House of Orange William Henry of Orange (William III) was born sovereign Prince of Orange, ruling over Holland, Utrecht, Zeeland and Guelders. Importantly he was a Protestant, and as a sign of their Protestant faith and their allegiance to the house of Orange many of his subjects chose displays of orange clothing, heraldry, and flags. When he and his wife Mary acceded to the thrones of England, Scotland and Ireland in 1689, orange was incorporated into the flags of Ireland (where it remains today) and of South Africa from 1928 to 1994.

Orange became such a statement of political allegiance that it was not allowed in gardens belonging to staunch Catholics; conversely, Protestants revelled in the cultivation of this new vegetable. Whether William III was presented with a bowl of root vegetables in shades of orange and decided to adopt them as a suitable emblem is not clear but it's a tantalising thought that without the powerful house of Orange our appreciation of the root vegetable may have assumed a different hue.

Witches' Broomsticks and Hedgerow Herbs

There are stories of witches flying on broomsticks dating back to the fifteenth century. The claim was made in 1453 in a confession by a male witch named Guillaume Edelin of St. Germain-en-Laye, near Paris; but he was not alone and throughout the 1500s there are many records of those claiming to fly and those claiming to have witnessed others fly. In his 1584 book *The Discoveries of Witchcraft* Reginald Scott writes of a ceremony in which assembled witches leap and dance singing, "Har, har, divell divell, dance here dance here, plaie here plaie here, Sabbath, Sabbath" while holding brooms aloft or between their legs.

There are images to reinforce the claims: in both *Le Champion des Dames* by Martin Lefranc dating from the 1440s and in frescoes in Schleswig Cathedral, Germany, images link brooms and witches, the latter twelfth-century wall painting showing Frigg, the Norse deity riding her staff.

With an intimate knowledge of plants, potions, cause and effect, herbalists, witches and the shamans prepared brews, lotions, salves and oils combining plant residue with animal fats with the specific aim of separating body from spirit. When applied to the body these plant-based potions were easily absorbed. "But the vulgar believe, and the witches confess, that on certain days or nights they anoint a staff and ride on it to the appointed place" is how Jordanes de Bergamo described it in his fifteenth-century writings. Details may be scarce on the concoctions that promoted early stories of flight, but a tour of the average rural hedgerow provides a wealth of hints.

Wild flowers such as Deadly Nightshade, Henbane, Wolfsbane and Mandrake to name a few are all potential candidates as they are rich in alkaloids, atropine, hyoscyamine and scopolamine, all known hallucinogenic compounds. Consume these plants internally and serious stomach discomforts can follow but external application to parts of the body rich in blood vessels or sweat glands ensures slow absorption, thus avoiding intestinal cramps.

So it seems that far from flying through the skies on their brooms the witches would simply 'trip' on herbs that made them think they were flying.

The Anti-Dandruff Hitchhiker and a Fizzy Drink

Any child who has ever roamed hedgerows and streamsides will be familiar with the Burdock (*Arctium lappa*), a giant of a plant with leathery rounded leaves and thistle-like blooms towering overhead. Once faded the flowers morph into cone-like structures composed of a thousand or more seeds, each with a miniature grappling hook. It is these seeds that provide their greatest appeal. Endless games follow as the 'burs' readily stick to any passing human or animal. This evolutionary tool for hitching a ride with migrating stock has served the plant well, allowing it to travel extensively throughout the Asian and European regions. It is so successful that many think of it as a weed.

Sufficiently enlightened to refrain from calling a successful coloniser a weed, ancient Chinese herbalists enlisted the plant's help for just about any kind of skin problem on the knees, lips, or tongue, and to cure leprosy, psoriasis, abscesses, acne, corns, warts, and dry skin. The Chinese also deduced some 3000 years ago that in addition to cleansing the skin, Burdock could combat problems with glands under the skin.

Peek into the plant in a laboratory and an extract of the root, found as an oil contains lignans including arctigenin, glycoside arctiin, and matairesinol; polyacetylenes including tridecadienetetraynes, tridecatrienetriynes; and a sulphur containing arctic acid. It also contains amino acids including alpha guanidino-n-butyric acid, inulin, organic acids, fatty acids, and phenolic acids. This rich bevy of compounds means that the oil offers antibacterial and anti-inflammatory properties and shows benefit when used externally in the treatment of psoriasis, dandruff, wounds, ulcers, eczema, boils, styes, sores and acne. Chinese researchers have also suggested that Burdock is anti-inflammatory, antipyretic, diuretic, antitumor, antifungal, estrogenic, hypoglycaemic, and antibacterial when taken internally.

In the West we have dragged our feet in deploying the plant's properties; in some parts of Europe it is customary to brew the root into a tea before either drinking it, or tipping it over your head. This rationale mirrors much of the Chinese herbalists' approach, reducing the effects of dandruff externally while cleansing the system internally. It is this crude brew that was enriched with the Dandelion (*Taraxacum officinale*) to create a potent blend of the Burdock's properties with those of the Dandelion, notably as a cooling herb with diuretic, laxative, and anti-rheumatic effects, stimulating liver function and improving digestion.

Ironically this purifying drink is the origin of the now popular sugar-rich carbonated drink 'Dandelion and Burdock' that has replaced health benefits with an armoury of flavourings, artificial colourings, and refined sugars.

147

Memories of children in nativity plays mumbling the names of the gifts from the Three Wise Men to the new-born Christ may create an air of uncertainty over their origin and precise purpose. Gold is relatively straightforward but Frankincense and Myrrh less so.

Highly desired and revered both products had to be imported as the plants from which they derive are not native to Palestine. Found in Arabia, Ethiopia, Somalia and India the Boswellia trees *B. carterii, B. papyrifera, or B. thurifera* provide Frankincense while the thorny shrub *Commiphora myrrha* provides Myrrh. An incision is made in the bark through which the sap weeps. This is allowed to harden to form a white, yellow or amber glass-like resin which historically is sold at exorbitant prices.

The religious uses of Frankincense and Myrrh are also often cited as both are essential and approved ingredients in the creation of the incense burned during church ceremonies. Historically, laws set out what could be burned in churches and the fragrance of Frankincense and Myrrh was said to emit a pleasant perfume that wafted up to God.

Aside from religious uses, Frankincense was burned as a mind relaxant, for its calming, soothing and purifying properties. Employed in creams and lotions it served as an antiseptic, healing wounds and also as a remedy for arthritic pains. It was also an essential ingredient in the embalming of bodies. However, the one contemporary universal practice for which Frankincense is responsible is the application of eyeliner. Traditionally it was the ash produced from this plant resin that was painted under the eyelid to beautify the wearers but, more importantly, to protect them from the evil eye.

Consumed in larger quantities in the United States than in all other countries together, Mustard is a condiment that was originally a medicine. It originates from two plants of the Cabbage family: Black Mustard (*Brassica nigra*), and White Mustard (*Sinapis alba*). First recorded as a cultivated plant in India around 3000 BC both species appear in the writings of Hippocrates in the form of Mustard paste to be used for muscular relief and to cure toothache. The name Mustard stems from the Latin *mustum ardens* or burning must, a reference to the heat of the paste when mixed with must (the unfermented grapes from which wine is made). It was this concoction that was widely prescribed for application to the head and chest to fight colds and fever.

Others chose to mix the Mustard powder with mutton fat, before applying it to the feet to cure aches, joint pain and even to stop frostbite. By the fifteenth century Mustard was commonly prescribed as a tonic. Icelandic herbalist Bjornsson wrote, "Mustard whets a man's wits, and it loosens the belly, breaks the stones, and purges the urine, if one eats Mustard, that strengthens the stomach and lessens its sickness.

Crushed mustard in vinegar heals viper's bite." In India it was common to sprinkle the powder in clothes to stave off the cold and to massage paste into the navel to enliven the spirit. Any or all of these uses could explain the reasoning behind Pope John XXII's creation in the early fourteenth century of the official Vatican position of *Grand moutardier du pape*, or Chief Mustard Maker to the Pope; or perhaps he simply liked the hotdogs of the day.

94 Flu and the German Snake Charmer

Lead by example may well have been the motto of a German born doctor in the late 1800s. He was so convinced of the efficacy of a treatment for snake bites that he offered to demonstrate it by allowing himself to be bitten by any snake. Thinking that he'd discovered a panacea for life while roaming the plains of North America, H.F. Meyer bullied the establishment into considering his idea but, unimpressed by the showman, the establishment simply stole his idea and in 1887 marketed Echinacea in medicinal form.

Meyer may have claimed to be the originator of the treatment but the native tribes of North America had a well established medicine chest based on this now popular garden flower. The Sioux applied it as a poultice against animal bites, the Cheyenne for sore mouths, the Choctaws for coughs, the Comanche for sore throats, the Crow for colds, the Kiowas for both sore throats and colds, and the Delaware for venereal diseases.

Although there are nine species of Echinacea, and many garden cultivars, the native tribes perfectly identified the most potent, *Echinacea angustifolia*, using only its roots, which is why one of the plant's common names is Snake Root. Early research suggested the plant possessed powers to speed up the removal of infection from the body; today it is known that it stimulates the production of lymphocytes, the white blood cells responsible for killing invaders, while also encouraging phagocytes, the white blood cells that combat infection.

Meyer never got to prove his theory but what he did achieve was to highlight one of the most potent of all herbal remedies for empowering the immune system to fight infection.

Supermarket in a Tree

Few plants can claim to work miracles but an unusual deciduous tree from the foothills of the Himalayas and north-west India offers such a blinding array of talents that it is now considered a major weapon in the worldwide fight against malnutrition.

Moringa oleifera has lived amongst indigenous people in northern India gathering a reputation for its health-giving properties but only recently have its real talents been understood. Fast growing and coming rapidly into flower and fruit it is adapted to arid, sandy conditions and heat, and flourishes in the most parched and testing areas of the globe. It is characterized by its corky bark, scrubby habit and pinnate foliage. White fragrant blooms are carried in sprays and seeds are held in pendulous pods, giving the plant its common name of Drumstick Tree.

While aesthetically it does little to inspire, medicinally and practically it is invaluable. It is used as a vegetable, a spice, and a source of cooking and cosmetic oil. All parts of the tree have medicinal properties and are used extensively against rheumatism, venomous bites, inflammation of the throat, bronchitis, piles, stomatitis, urinary infections, asthma, eye diseases, heart complaints, inflammation, dyspepsia, and muscle diseases. It is also a circulatory stimulant, a laxative, an expectorant, a diuretic, and, of course, an aphrodisiac.

Nutritionally the statistics are staggering. It is claimed that, weight for weight, it contains three times more iron than Spinach, seven times the vitamin C of Oranges, three times the potassium of Bananas, four times more calcium than milk, four times more vitamin A than Carrots, and as much protein as eggs. And if you have eaten abroad in Burma, the Philippines, Maldives, India, or Thailand you have probably consumed it unknowingly in stews, sauces, and curries as it is a staple addition to many dishes.

Perhaps as important as the nutritional advantages are the water cleansing properties of the seeds. When ground to a powder, mixed with water and allowed to settle for an hour the water is cleared of sediment and stripped of up to 99% of waterborne bacteria.

Henry and the 57 Horseradish

In 1869 when the parents of a young boy called Henry offered to fuel his curiosity by providing him with a patch of land on which to grow some plants, few could have anticipated the results, especially as the only crop he grew was Horseradish (*Amoracia rusticana*).

Said to be a mispronunciation of 'harsh radish' the common name says much of the plant's taste characteristics and with the Latin radix meaning 'root' there is no doubt which part of the plant is consumed. It was once hugely valued: the Oracle at Delphi is said to have told Apollo that, "The radish is worth its weight in lead, the beet its weight in silver, the horseradish its weight in gold." A member of the Cabbage family, it is closely related to Mustard. The same compounds in each tickle and excite the taste buds. But the heat generated was first used to treat rheumatism, gout, flu and bronchial complaints by binding the pulverised flesh of the root to the affected skin with cloth. It then progressed as a wormer for

cattle and horses, as the basis for cough medicine, and somewhere in history found itself declared a potent aphrodisiac. The famed bite and odour of the plant are released only when the root is grated to release a volatile oil known as allyl isothiocyanate. The addition of vinegar stems their release so those of a sensitive disposition should opt for horseradish products high in vinegar.

Interesting though the uses of Horseradish are there can have been little presentiment that young Henry would ever turn a profit from his labours in his Horseradish patch, but fortunately his parents supported his enterprise as the company he set up was called H.J. Heinz. Today Horseradish is once again exciting scientists as biochemists have found that an enzyme called Horseradish Peroxidase acts as a marker that highlights particular molecules. It has proved particularly valuable in modern research on the nervous system and in biopsies for cancer.

Fennel Mystery

The popularity of a plant usually ensures a long and varied cultivation down the centuries. Remain in favour and a place in cultivation is almost guaranteed with the determination and ingenuity of humans overcoming considerable odds to ensure supply. One plant that gained sufficient attention to warrant Pliny the Elder describing it as "one of the most precious gifts from nature to man", is a wild relative of the Fennel, commonly called Silphium, not to be confused with the genus of the same name. Naturalised on a narrow strip of land on the coastal plateau of Cyrene, an area now part of Libya, this lofty plant displayed clusters of yellow blooms on top of ribbed, thick, fleshy stems. The plant was in such demand that the city of Cyrene became one of the key trading posts of the early Roman period. We are told that, to the Romans, the plant was worth its weight in silver coins. It even appeared on the coins of Cyrene, then a Greek colony. Textual references of the period depict an impressive portfolio of uses, from food seasoning to medication. The flowers were used in perfumes, the young stems for human consumption, older ones for cattle fodder, while juices formed the base of medications for aches,

seizures, indigestion, fever, bronchial and flu symptoms, wart removal, leprosy and even as a hair restorer. Trade was understandably brisk for such a panacea, enhanced by unusual horticultural characteristics that resulted in the plant failing to transplant to other areas and not responding to cultivation. Diligently the Cyrenians imposed strict rules on harvests in attempts to maintain supply and prices. Such measures might have been effective had it not been for the widespread use of Silphium resin, the dried and crystallised sap, as a contraceptive. To the sexually liberated Romans the drug was ubiquitous, grains of sap being ground with nuts, diluted in alcohol or blended with garlic before consumption. Pliny suggested that *laser* or *laserpicium*, the specific name of the resin, be taken monthly to 'promote discharge', the drug possibly acting as an abortifacient. Research in the latter decades of the twentieth century has demonstrated the theoretical viability of the recipes while more recent applications of similar plants

have proved 100% effective in animals. The consensus is that the compounds present in it could block progesterone, essential if the uterus wall is to retain the foetus. If true, the Romans popularised the most effective natural birth control known. Botanists hypothesise about this mystery plant, known only by its common name, with some suggesting that *Ferula tingitana*, a wild Fennel that has shown some migration into North Africa, matches the profile.

Unfortunately conclusive evidence escapes us as the plant was described as extinct in the first century AD, the last piece apparently being eaten by the Emperor Nero, quite why is not recorded! Dwindling plant exports and two devastating earthquakes in the region left Cyrene in ruins. It remains today only as an archaeological site.

98
Sweet Cherries

A willing participant at many banquets King Henry VIII of England is said by John Aubrey to have first tasted cherries in Flanders. Clearly enamoured with the sweet fruits, he had cherry trees shipped to England for cultivation. When he subsequently tasted the fruit grown in Kent, Henry, clearly delighted with his culinary contribution, proclaimed the county the 'Garden of England'.

The nomenclature and folklore of some plants paints a dreamy picture of a rural idyll; none more so than Dipsacus, the Teasel. Derived from the Greek, it translates as 'a little cup of water'. Where the leaves merge, a small cup is formed and it was said that if young girls gathered the pure dew that collected there they would have eternal youth. The story is spoiled somewhat when the treatment of acne and warts and the removal of facial hair are also spoken of.

The common name, Teasel, is derived from the Anglo Saxon, literally meaning to tease or prise apart hair, cloth or fibre. It is for this purpose that the Teasel was enlisted commercially. Fuller's Teasel, a branching subspecies was used as a comb for raising the nap in fabrics, most notably felts for the millinery trade.

Known as the world's rarest coffee Kopi Luwak is described as having a delicate flavour with all bitterness removed. It is a drink revered by connoisseurs and is sold at premium prices.

The coffee fruit is ingested by *Paradoxurus hermaphroditus*, the Asian Palm Civet, a mongoose-like creature that enjoys the flesh but excretes the coffee beans, which are diligently collected by locals who prepare and package them for sale.

Dynamic, passionate and hugely creative, Chris Beardshaw is one of the leading lights in the world of gardening. On screen and on air, he is loved by millions for his ability to communicate and share his rich vein of knowledge with warmth and enthusiasm. Off screen he is equally admired for his huge variety of work in design and education, where he is recognised as a real ambassador for the industry.

As a young adult Chris trained and worked in horticulture but it was his love of art and design that led to a degree and postgraduate studies in Landscape Architecture, making him one of the few presenters who combines both disciplines. His connection with people and ability to communicate were picked up by a leading horticultural college, his love of teaching soon became evident and he started to lecture full-time in Horticulture, Garden Design and Garden History.

He remains passionate about education and works hard to combine his other commitments with teaching. He has developed close working relationships with educational institutions around the country including The Royal Botanic Garden Edinburgh, The Duchy College and Birmingham City University. He is a Trustee of Capel Manor College.

Chris heads up a private design practice and has undertaken design and consultancy roles on a number of high profile projects for clients such as English Heritage, the RSPB, the RNLI and Jodrell Bank Discovery Centre. Chris sees a garden as a dynamic and transient work of art and his open-minded approach to design is one of the reasons that make so many major organisations choose to work with him.

He is also a regular columnist on magazines and journals including *The English Garden* and *Garden News*, and is the author of three books.

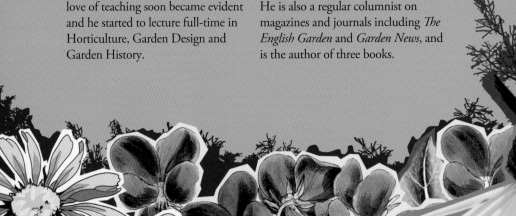

Chris Beardshaw

Chris constantly proves his breadth and depth of knowledge of not just horticulture but history, science and the natural world. His broadcasting experience includes solo and co-presenting roles as well as live broadcasts and news reports - programmes include: *Apples: British to the Core* - BBC4, *Wild About Your Garden* - BBC1, *Ploughs, Cows & Clover* - BBC2, *The Flying Gardener* - BBC2, *Gardeners' World* - BBC2, *Hidden Gardens* - BBC2, *Great Garden Detectives* - ITV, *Country Lives* – ITV and many more. He is also a long-standing and regular panel member of BBC Radio 4's popular *Gardeners' Question Time*. Being a panel member is not for the faint-hearted but Chris enjoys nothing more than being put on the spot by a live audience.

THE END

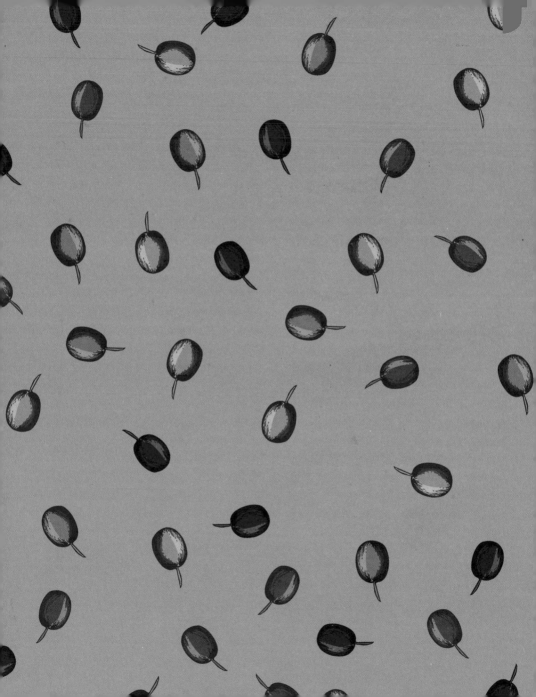